First Grade
FOUNDATIONS

GRADE 1

American Education Publishing™
An imprint of Carson-Dellosa Publishing LLC
Greensboro, North Carolina

American Education Publishing™
An imprint of Carson-Dellosa Publishing LLC
P.O. Box 35665
Greensboro, NC 27425 USA

ISBN 978-1-62399-077-0

02-147137784

Table Of Contents

Table Of Contents

Table Of Contents

Table Of Contents

First grade is all about expanding on the basic skills your child learned in preschool and kindergarten. Your first grader will also begin to work on social skills such as paying attention, working with others on group projects, and gaining confidence in sharing opinions.

In first grade, an emphasis is placed on the more academic skills of language arts and math. By completing this workbook, your child will not only be mastering these skills, but also building confidence and the desire to learn.

First Grade Foundations offers activities for a full year of practice. The practice pages are simple and engaging, providing hours of learning fun. Many activities also connect with science or social studies for a wide range of learning. With *First Grade Foundations*, your child is getting a well-rounded supplement to his or her education.

Language Arts

As a first grader, your child will begin to demonstrate command of the conventions of standard English grammar and usage when writing and speaking. With *First Grade Foundations*, he or she will gain more of an exposure of the English language, and with more exposure will come greater confidence and understanding.

In first grade, your child will learn:

• to identify the main topic and retell key details of a text. **pages 64-65**
• to use singular and plural nouns. **pages 81-84**
• to use verbs and adjectives. **pages 85-88**
• to capitalize dates and names of people. **page 89**
• to use end punctuation for sentences. **pages 90-91**

A strong understanding of language arts will help your child in learning how to read. In first grade, your child will practice reading comprehension of age-appropriate texts. Reading also stimulates your child's imagination and encourages creativity, as well as building language skills. Here are fun ways to expose your child to a love of learning:

• Encourage your child to tell you about his or her day. Write each event of your child's day on a separate strip of paper as he or she relates them to you. Then, cut the strips apart, and challenge your child to rearrange the events in the correct order.

- Watch the news with your child and discuss the job of a news reporter. After your child understands what reporters do, create your own newscast. You can be the reporter, and you child can pretend to be a character from a book or movie. Make up the questions together, and use them for an "interview."

Math

As a first grader, your child will be focusing on four key areas: addition and subtraction within 20, place value, measurement, and shapes. With *First Grade Foundations*, your child will practice math skills that are fundamental to learning these concepts. These skills will provide building blocks for the years of schooling to come.

In first grade, your child will learn:

- to count to 100. **pages 98–100**
- addition and subtraction within 20. **pages 116–124, 129–130, 167–172**
- place value of hundreds, tens, and ones. **pages 141–143**
- to distinguish between 2-dimensional and 3-dimensional shapes. **pages 144–145**
- to tell and write time. **pages 152–154**
- to measure and compare lengths. **pages 155–158**

Your child will become more interested in math if he or she can see how it applies to life outside of school. Here are fun ways to practice age-appropriate math with your child throughout each day:

- Let your child practice "trading" with pennies and dimes to reinforce the concepts of ones and tens. Roll a die and let your child take as many pennies from the "pot" as the die indicates. When he or she has 10 pennies, he or she can trade them in for a dime.
- Use dry beans or other small objects to practice counting. Have your child divide 10 beans into two separate groups and combine them by adding. Then, have your child write the number problem on paper and read it to you.

d b f

Long i

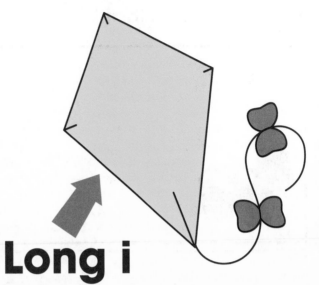

The Sound Connection

Directions: Draw a line to match each letter with the picture whose name begins with that letter sound.

b   d   f   g

q   v   w   z

Draw a picture of something with a name that begins with each letter shown.

h   p   t

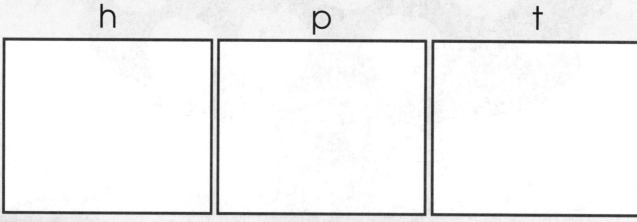

Say the name of each picture you drew. Write the letter of the final sound for each word.

10

Circle That Sound

Directions: Say the name of each picture. Circle the letter that makes the beginning sound. In the last row, write the letter that makes the beginning sound.

t z s	s c p	p m t
r b f	v y w	d b f

Write a secret message using pictures instead of letters. Draw pictures with names that have the same beginning sounds as the letters in the word or words you are writing.

Sounds the Same

Directions: Color the pictures in each row with names that begin with the same sound as the letter shown. In the final box, draw a picture or write a word that begins with the same letter.

b

d

g

m

Try This!

Write the letter of the final sound for each word above.

Hear It Last

Directions: Say the name of each picture. Circle the letter that makes the final sound.

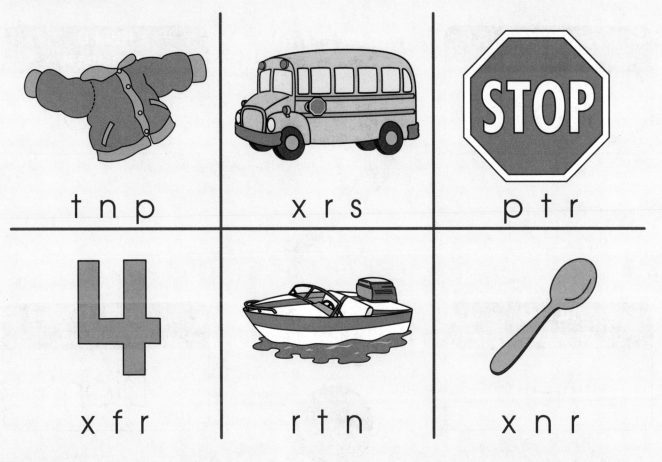

t n p	x r s	p t r
x f r	r t n	x n r

Directions: Say the name of each picture. Write the letter that makes the final sound.

_____ _____ _____

Try This!

On another sheet of paper, write three sentences using at least three of the above words.

Fun with Final Sounds

Directions: Say the name of each picture and each name. Draw a line to match each picture to the name with the same final sound.

HELLO
my name is

Scott

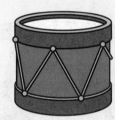

HELLO
my name is

Taylor

HELLO
my name is

Nell

HELLO
my name is

Dion

HELLO
my name is

Nick

HELLO
my name is

Sam

Try This!

On another sheet of paper, list five words that end with the same final sound as your first name.

Show What You Know

Directions: Say the name of each picture. Write the first and last letters of each word. Color the pictures with names that have the same vowel sound as **bat**. Circle the pictures with names that have the same vowel sound as **top**.

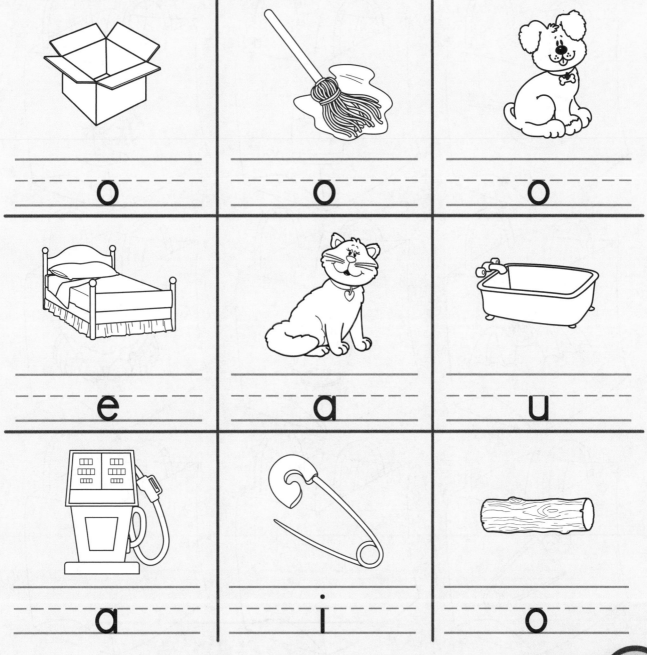

o   o   o

e   a   u

a   i   o

Try This!

On another sheet of paper, write the above words in **ABC** order.

15

Bag of Vowels

Directions: Say the name of each picture. Color the pictures with the **short a** sound. On each empty bag, draw a picture of something with a name that has the **short a** sound.

Try This!

Draw a circle around each picture with the **short i** sound.

All Cracked Up

Directions: Cut out the puzzle pieces. Put the puzzle together and glue it on a separate sheet of paper. Say the name of each picture. Color the eggs with the **short e** sound.

Try This!

On the back of your completed puzzle, list 10 **short e** words. Circle any words that rhyme.

17

Hear the Vowel

Directions: Say the name of each picture. Fill in the circle for the letter of the short vowel sound. Color the pictures that have the **short i** sound.

○ a ○ i ○ u	○ e ○ i ○ o	○ a ○ i ○ u
○ i ○ o ○ u	○ a ○ e ○ o	○ a ○ e ○ i
○ i ○ e ○ u	○ a ○ i ○ u	○ e ○ i ○ o

Top of the Box

Directions: Unscramble the letters to name each picture. Color the pictures with the **short o** sound.

b d e

p m o

o t p

a m n

r c k o

c k l o

Choose one short o word from above.
List some words that rhyme with the word.

Gus and His Drum

Directions: Help Gus find his drum. Find a path through the words that have the **short u** sound.

bus

dug

nut

truck

gum

mug

bag

rug

ant

pin

duck

egg

hat

top

pan

big

hug

up

ten

plug

tug

luck

brush

cup

On another sheet of paper, sort all of the words from the maze by vowel sounds.

21

What Am I?

Directions: Circle the name of each picture.

fin
fan
fun

can
ran
sand

crab
crib
web

pan
pen
pin

crab
crib
pet

pan
pen
pin

fence
fan
fish

mat
mitt
men

mat
mitt
men

mitt
men
man

Try This!

Draw circles around the pictures with names that rhyme.

All Aboard!

Directions: Cut out the words. Glue each word on the train car with the matching picture. Write your own **long a** words in the empty train cars.

hay | snake | cave | rain | vase | nail

Seek and See

Directions: Circle all of the **long e** words. Draw a line to match each sentence to the correct picture.

Jean sees a key in the tree.

Dean reads a book about seas.

Will she eat meat or beans?

What did he see in the stream?

Pete had a dream about sheep.

Try This!

On another sheet of paper, write a poem that has at least three **long e** words. Draw a picture to go with your poem.

25

Long i Art

Directions: Follow the directions. Circle the words that have the **long i** sound.

Draw a hive for the bees.

Draw a prize for the knight.

Draw stripes on the kite.

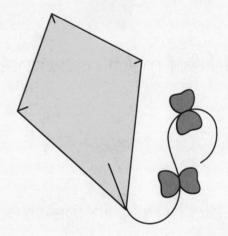

Color nine ties.

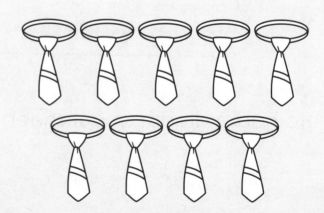

On another sheet of paper, write a sentence that has two **long i** words.
Draw a picture to go with your sentence.

Give a Dog a Bone

Directions: Color the bones with words that have the **long o** sound. Write **long o** words in the empty bones.

comb

cone

pot

log

nose

clock

rose

mop

hose

Try This!

Circle the bones with words that rhyme.

Rows of Cubes

Directions: Color the cube blue if the picture's name has the **long u** sound. Circle the row that has the most **long u** pictures.

On another sheet of paper, draw three ice cubes.
Draw pictures or write words that have the **long u** sound.

No Place Like Home

Directions: Use the code to color the homes.

long a = red	**long i** = orange	**long u** = blue
long e = green	**long o** = yellow	

goat   mice

Friends Way

crow   park

Friends Way

lion   bee

Park Place

toad   snake

Park Place

firehouse

Firehouse Drive

mule   tiger

Firehouse Drive

Main Street

Try This!

On another sheet of paper, write directions from the goat's home to the firehouse.

29

Happy About Y

Directions: Write **y** to complete each word. If the **y** has the **long e** sound, color the happy face 😊. If the **y** has the **long i** sound, color the sad face ☹.

bab ____

fl ____

berr ____

funn ____

tr ____

b ____ e

On another sheet of paper, sort the above words by the **long i** and the **long e** sounds.

Basket of Vowels

Directions: Use the code to color the apples.

| long-vowel words = red | short-vowel words = yellow |

Count how many of the above words have short vowels.
Draw that same number of clouds in the sky.

31

Flower Power

Directions: Use the code to color the flowers. In the empty flower, draw a picture with a name that begins with **pl**.

bl words = blue   **cl** words = green   **fl** words = red

 **Try This!**

On another sheet of paper, draw a flower with six large petals.
In each petal, draw or write a word that begins with **bl**, **cl**, **fl**, or **pl**.

Get Your Head in the Clouds

Directions: Write the letters you hear at the beginning of each word. Use the code to color the clouds.

gl = gray   **pl** = blue

_ _ _ ant

_ _ _ ue

_ _ _ um

_ _ _ ove

_ _ _ ate

_ _ _ ug

Try This!

On another sheet of paper, write the above words in **ABC** order.

Friends Get Together

Directions: Write **cr**, **fr**, **gr**, **pr**, or **tr** to complete each word. Use the picture to answer the questions.

1. Does the _____incess have a _____own? YES NO

2. Does the _____ow have a _____ayon? YES NO

3. Did the _____incess win the _____ize? YES NO

4. Does the _____andma have a _____oom? YES NO

5. Is the _____og on the _____ill? YES NO

6. Is the _____ab in the _____uck? YES NO

On another sheet of paper, write a story about the picture above.

Star Blends

Directions: Write the blend that comes at the beginning of each word.

_ __ider

_ _ __arf

_ __ing

_ _ _ op

_ _ __ail

_ __ide

Directions: Draw a picture in each empty star that begins with an **s** blend.

Try This!

Cut out the stars and glue them to another sheet of paper in **ABC** order.

35

The Right Kite

Directions: Color the kites with words that rhyme.

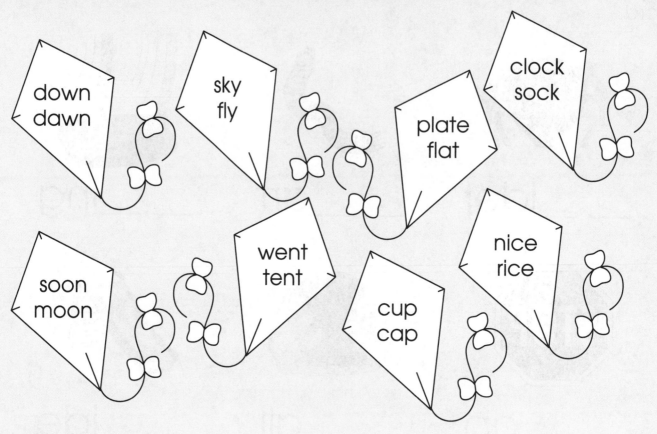

Directions: Write a rhyming word below each kite.

Try This!

Write a word on a piece of paper. Your friend then writes a rhyming word.
Continue playing until you run out of words. The last person to write a rhyming word wins.

Frogs in a Pond

Directions: Cut out the frogs. Glue each frog beside the lily pad with the rhyming word.

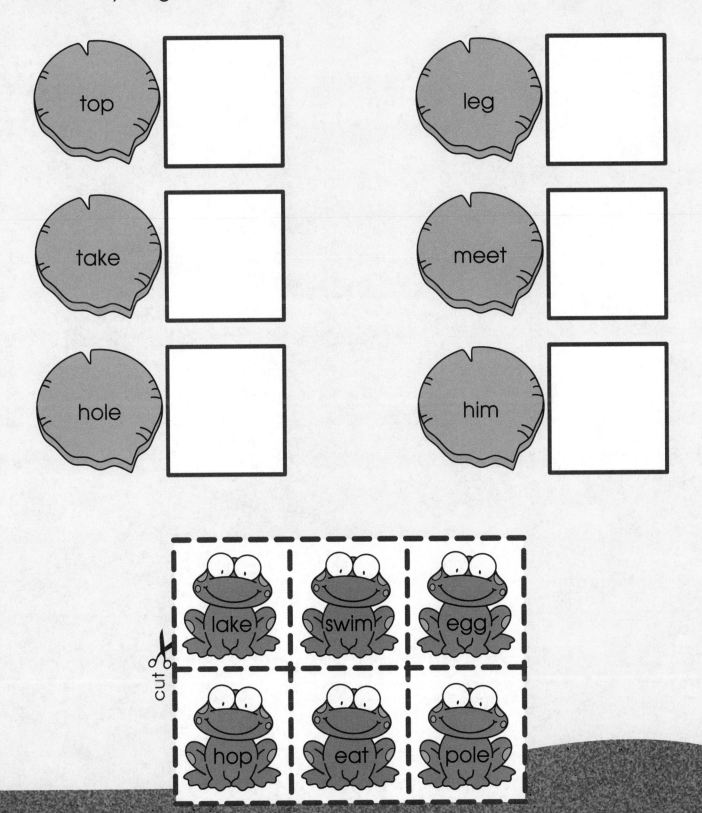

Theo's Flower Garden Path

Directions: Cut out the pictures. Glue the pictures whose names begin with the **/th/** sound on Theo's path.

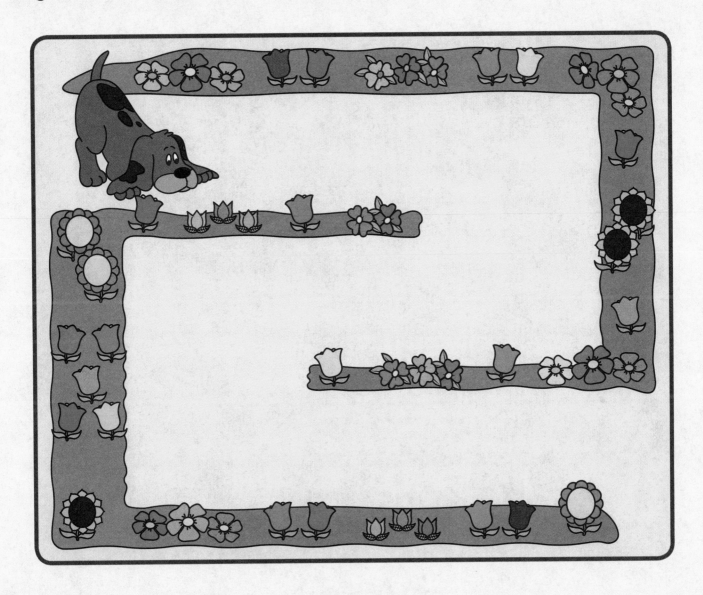

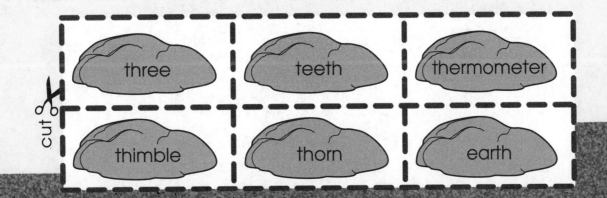

| three | teeth | thermometer |
| thimble | thorn | earth |

cut

Shells on the Seashore

Directions: Say the name of each picture. Use the code to color the shells.

> words that begin with the **/sh/** sound = pink
> words that end with the **/sh/** sound = brown
> words that do not have the **/sh/** sound = yellow

Directions: In this shell, draw a picture of something that has the **/sh/** sound in its name. Use the code to color the shell.

Try This!

On another sheet of paper, draw pictures of three things you might see at the beach that have the /sh/ sound in their names. Write the name of each picture.

Listen to the Fish

Directions: Use the code to color the fish.

ch = yellow   **sh** = red   **th** = green   **wh** = brown

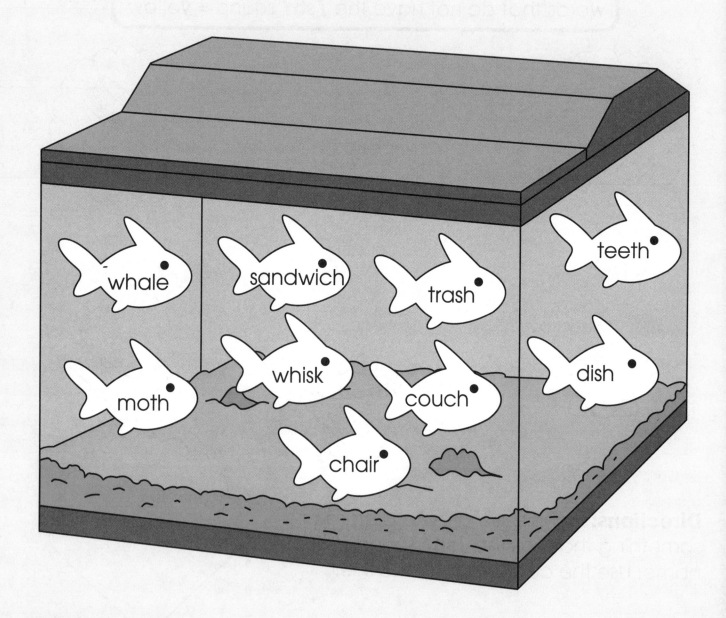

whale

sandwich

trash

teeth

moth

whisk

couch

dish

chair

Try This!

Draw three living things on another sheet of paper.

Ring and Sing

Directions: Write the letters **ng** to complete each word. Find and circle the words in the word search.

1. wro _____

2. bri _____

3. ra _____

4. stro _____

5. stu _____

6. wi _____

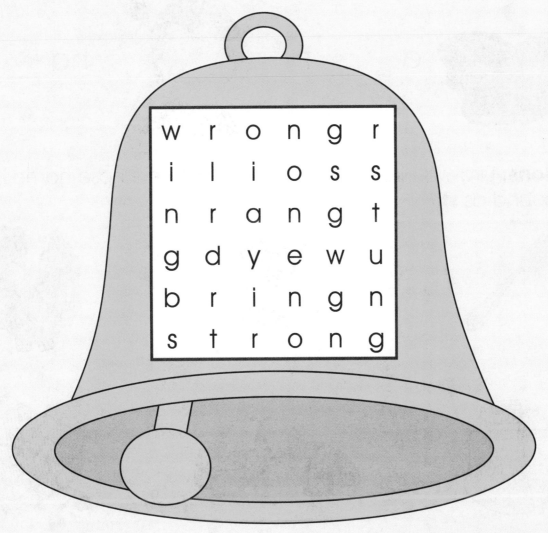

```
w  r  o  n  g  r
i  l  i  o  s  s
n  r  a  n  g  t
g  d  y  e  w  u
b  r  i  n  g  n
s  t  r  o  n  g
```

Try This!

Use construction paper to make a book of **ng** words. Cut the paper in half and staple the pages to make a book. On each page, draw a picture of a word that ends with **ng**.

Stirring Up Vowels

Directions: Write the letters **ir** to complete each word.

 sk __ __ t

 sh __ __ t

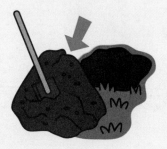 d __ __ t

 ha __ __

Directions: Draw a circle around each picture whose name has the same sound as **stir**.

Try This!

For each picture not circled, write the r-controlled vowel sound you hear.
Then, write at least two more r-controlled vowel sound words.

44

Ready for More

Directions: Circle the letters **or** in each word. Draw a line to match each word to the correct picture.

porch

acorn

storm

cord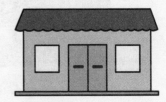

stork

store

corn

horn

On another sheet of paper, write the above words in **ABC** order.

45

On Mother's Day

Directions: Circle the correct word to complete each sentence.
Write the words on the lines.

Mother's Day is celebrated _____ the month of May.

up   **on**   **in**

I give my mom a kiss _____ her cheek.

up   **on**   **in**

We put flowers _____ a vase.

up   **on**   **in**

We hold _____ our sign.

up   **on**   **in**

Try This!

Use construction paper to make a Mother's Day card. Write a message that includes all three directional words above.

Let's Go Home

Directions: Cut out the animal pictures. Glue each picture on the correct house to show how many syllables are in the word.

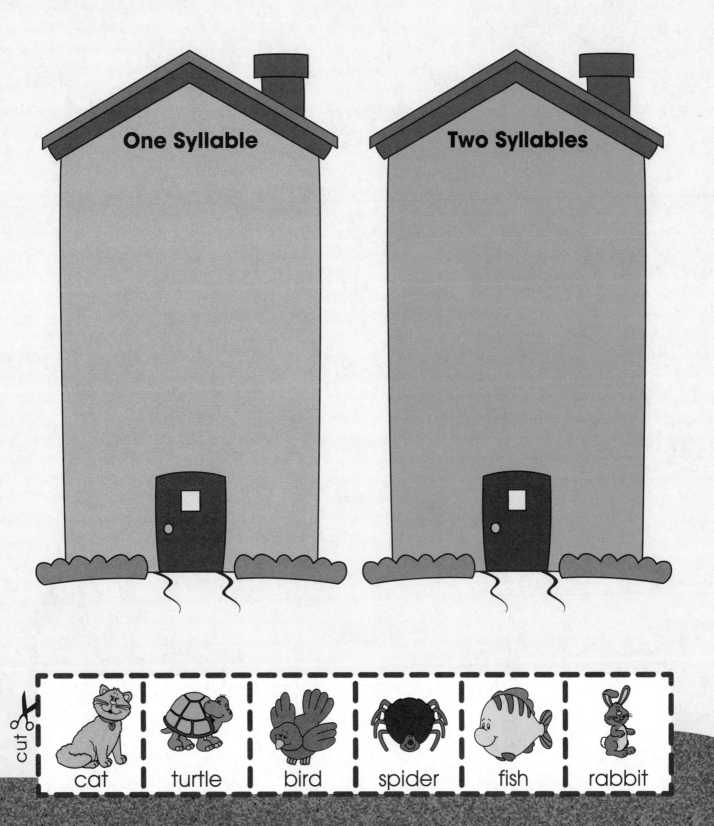

One Syllable

Two Syllables

cut

cat | turtle | bird | spider | fish | rabbit

Study and Learn with Synonyms

Directions: Draw lines to match the synonyms.

loud   sloppy

neat   laugh

giggle   noisy

messy   tidy

Directions: Cut out the pictures. Glue to match the synonyms.

happy	ill

angry	below

under

glad

mad

sick

cut

49

Antonyms Are All Around

Directions: Cut and glue to match the antonyms.

in

little

hard

cold

back

empty

front

out

full

big

hot

soft

For the Love of Words

Directions: Cut out the heart halves. Glue the heart halves next to the words that make compound words. Write the compound words on the lines.

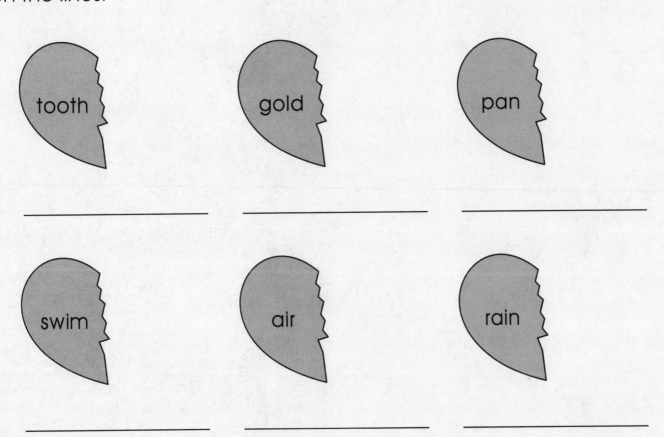

tooth   gold   pan

_____   _____   _____

swim   air   rain

_____   _____   _____

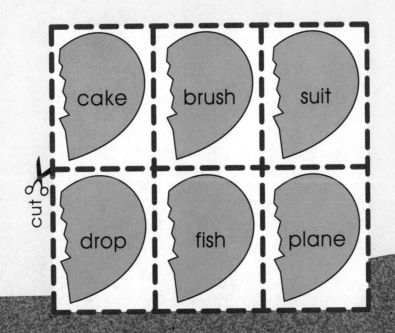

cake   brush   suit

drop   fish   plane

cut

I'll Brush My Teeth

Directions: Write the contraction from the word bank to complete each sentence.

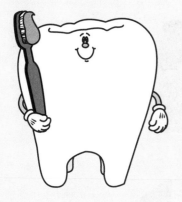

He'll	I'll
I'm	I've
She's	We're

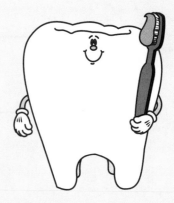

1. (We are) _____ going to the dentist today.

2. (I will) _____ brush my teeth before bed.

3. (She is) _____ going to floss her teeth.

4. (I am) _____ not going to eat too much sugar.

5. (He will) _____ get a cavity if he does not take care of his teeth.

6. (I have) _____ never had a cavity.

Use construction paper to create your own dental health poster. Write some things you should do every day to keep your teeth healthy, such as brush and floss.

Busy Birds

Directions: Write **1** in front of the picture that comes first. Write **2** in front of the picture that comes next. Write **3** in front of the picture that comes last.

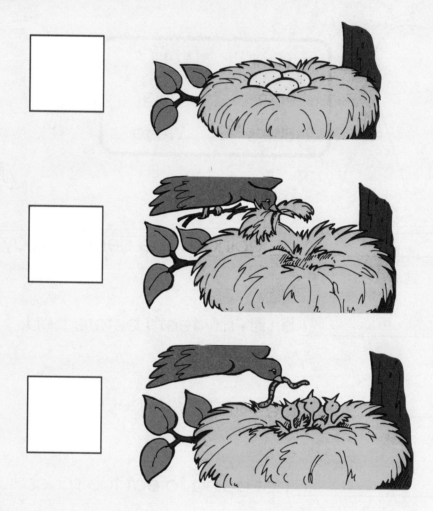

Directions: What do you think will happen next? Draw your answer in the box.

Try This!

On another sheet of paper, draw and number the steps you go through to get ready for school each day.

Mixed-Up Story

Directions: Cut out the pictures. Glue them on a separate sheet of paper in the right order to tell a story. Write a title for the story.

He rode his bike to the park.

He put his new bike away.

cut

He rode back home.

Wow! Thanks!

Logan got a new bike.

Try This!

Draw a map that shows all of the places Logan will ride his bike to. Remember to show the park and his house.

Life on the Farm

Directions: Follow the directions.

1. Color the dog brown.
2. Draw a fish in the pond.
3. Draw a box around the cow.
4. Circle the barn.
5. Color the hen yellow.
6. Draw an apple in the tree.

Label everything in the picture.

To the Moon!

Directions: Follow the directions.

1. If the moon is made of snow, write an **s**. _____

If it is made of rock, write an **r**. _____

2. If men have walked on the moon, write an **o**. _____

If an old man lives on the moon, write a **b**. _____

3. If the moon always looks round, write an **s**. _____

If it does not, write a **w**. _____

Directions: Write your letters on the lines to spell a word. The same word will fit in all of the blanks.

_____ _____ _____

           1   2   3

Pretty maids all in a _____.

_____, _____, _____ your boat.

Try This!

On another sheet of paper, list three things you would find in space other than the moon.

B Is for Blueberry

Directions: Cut out the pictures. Glue each picture where it belongs. Write the numbers **1** to **4** in the boxes to show the order that the blueberries grow.

The blueberries are in the basket.

The ladybug is on the sprout.

The butterfly is on the blueberry bush.

The seeds are in her hand.

cut

61

Web Spinners

Directions: Read the paragraph. Answer the questions.

> There are many kinds of spiders. Spiders have eight legs. They like to eat insects. Many spiders spin webs. The web is the spider's home. Have you ever seen a spiderweb?

Spiders have _____ legs.

        eight   four

A spider spins a _____.

       web   week

The web is a spider's _____.

      home   kite

What do spiders eat? ☐ insects   ☐ jelly

Draw eight legs on this spider.
Draw a web for this spider.

Where have you seen a spider build a web?
Draw a picture of a spiderweb you have seen.

We Like to Play

Directions: Read the stories. Write the main idea of each story.

Joe went to the park. He went down the slide. He had lunch on a picnic table. He went on the swings after lunch.

_____

Tara wore a princess dress. She put on a crown. She looked in the mirror. Tara loves to play dress-up.

_____

Try This!

Choose one of the stories above and continue the story on another sheet of paper.

Bear Is Busy

Directions: Circle **true** if the sentence tells about the picture. Circle **false** if it does not.

true   false

1. It is a very hot day.

true   false

2. The hat is too small.

true   false

3. The bear walks to school.

true   false

4. The bear washed three shirts.

Work with a friend to practice finding the main idea. Each person draws a picture. Swap papers. Above the picture, write the main idea of the picture.

Can You Believe It?

Directions: Read each sentence. If the sentence tells something that could really happen, check **nonfiction**. If the sentence tells something that is make-believe, check **fiction**.

	Fiction	Nonfiction
1. A bear can live in a forest.	◯	◯
2. A bear can search in a store for a lost button.	◯	◯
3. A bear can sew a button on a shirt.	◯	◯
4. A bear can catch a fish.	◯	◯
5. A bear can talk to a girl.	◯	◯
6. A bear can have a cub.	◯	◯
7. A bear can climb a tree.	◯	◯
8. A bear and a puppy can be friends.	◯	◯
9. A bear sleeps in a bed.	◯	◯

Try This!

Write the titles of five books. Sort the titles into fiction and nonfiction books. Ask a friend to check your work.

Be Earth's Friend

Directions: Write the word from the word bank to complete each sentence.

cans	clothes	groceries
off	running	

1. I bring my _____ home in reusable cloth bags.

2. We put our empty soft drink _____ in the recycling bin.

3. You should turn _____ the lights when you leave the room.

4. My mom gives my _____ to charity when they are too small.

5. Don't leave the water _____ when brushing your teeth.

Try This!

Draw a circle by the sentence if it tells about recycling. Draw a square by the sentence if it tells about reusing. Draw a triangle by the sentence if it tells about reducing.

A Dog's Life

Directions: Circle the word that correctly completes each sentence.

1. Dogs have been around for a _____ time.

   men   long   him

2. _____ are more than 400 kinds of dogs.

   There   From   This

3. Dogs _____ us in many ways.

   word   that   help

4. Dogs _____ work.

   be   more   can

Directions: Reorder the words to make a sentence.

   play   will   Some   fetch.   dogs

_____

Make a dog care poster.
On construction paper, draw or write five things that people can do to take care of dogs.

Fun Fox Facts

Directions: Read the paragraph. Answer the questions.

A fox can live in the woods, near a farm, or in the desert. Foxes can even live in the city. They run fast. They hunt for what they eat. They can have red, gray, or white fur. A baby fox is called a **kit**. A fox's home is called a **den**.

1. Name two places a fox can live.

_____   _____

2. What colors of fur can foxes have?

_____   _____   _____

3. How does a fox get food? _____

4. What is a fox home called? _____

Use a sheet of construction paper to make a fox information poster. Draw a picture of a fox and write four to five facts on the poster.

Packing Day for David

Directions: Read the story. Answer the questions.

> David has to move. His family found a new home in the city. David has to pack all of his toys. He will give away the old toys. He will place the newer toys in a big box.

1. Where did David's family find a new home?

_____

_____

2. What will he do with his newer toys?

_____

_____

3. What will he do with his old toys?

_____

_____

On another sheet of paper, tell about a time you gave away a toy.

Which Pet?

Directions: Read each sentence. If the sentence tells how dogs and cats are the same, write **S** on the line. If the sentence tells how dogs and cats are different, write **D** on the line.

1. Dogs and cats are animals. _____

2. Dogs bark, and cats meow. _____

3. Dogs and cats have four feet. _____

4. Dogs like to chew, and cats like to scratch. _____

5. Dogs and cats can be good pets. _____

Directions: Write your own sentence about how dogs and cats are different.

_____

_____

Think of a friend or a family member. On another sheet of paper, write two ways you are the same and two ways you are different.

Out in the Cold

Directions: Write **C** in front of each sentence that tells about the cause. Write **E** in front of each sentence that tells about the effect. Write and label your own cause-and-effect sentence for number 4.

1. _____ Tom was cold.

   _____ He rubbed his hands together.

2. _____ The rubbing made his hands warm.

   _____ He rubbed his hands harder.

3. _____ He rubbed his hands faster.

   _____ That made his hands hot.

4. _____ Tom _____.

   _____ _____.

On another sheet of paper, write about a time when you were cold. What caused you to feel cold? What did you do?

72

Tell Me Why

Directions: Read each pair of words. Which one is the cause? Which one is the effect? Write the words on the correct lines.

1. rain, wet

cause _____   effect _____

2. hot, sun

cause _____   effect _____

3. plant, seed

cause _____   effect _____

Directions: Write a cause-and-effect sentence that uses one set of words from above.

_____

_____

On another sheet of paper, write three causes and their effects.

Fun at the Zoo

Directions: Circle the ending that makes sense.

1. Jade's class was going on a trip. They were going to the zoo.

A big bus came to get them.

They all went home.

They got on the bus.

They went out to play.

2. They rode for a long time. Then, the bus came to a stop.

They were at the zoo!

They all got off the bus.

They went to the store.

They got on top of the bus.

Directions: Write an ending that makes sense.

They went into the zoo. They went to see the lion.
He had a big mane. He had big teeth.

_____

_____

On another sheet of paper, list 15 animals you would see at the zoo.

Anna Is on Time!

Directions: Cut out the sentences. Glue each sentence under the correct picture.

Anna's alarm clock rings.

Anna picks up her books.

Anna is getting hungry.

Anna hears the school bell ring.

✂ cut

It is time to get up.

It is time to go to school.

It is time to go home from school.

It is time to eat lunch.

Sort Them Out

Directions: Circle the name of the animal that does not belong in each group. Write the letters beside the circled words to solve the riddle.

Birds

1. L robin
   N bluebird
   I cow
   J crow

Insects

2. L snake
   A ladybug
   N wasp
   T bee

Dogs

3. B collie
   I beagle
   S shepherd
   L ox

Reptiles

4. R snake
   I horse
   G turtle
   W alligator

Farm Animals

5. G tiger
   K pig
   O cow
   Y hen

Jungle Animals

6. J lion
   B cheetah
   U tiger
   A rat

Zoo Animals

7. M bear
   O giraffe
   T dog
   F zebra

Ocean Animals

8. H octopus
   T whale
   K shark
   O camel

Fish

9. R raccoon
   I salmon
   V catfish
   L tuna

What do you call a sick crocodile?

An "___ ___ ___ ___ ___ ___ ___ ___ ___"
    1   2   3   4   5   6   7   8   9

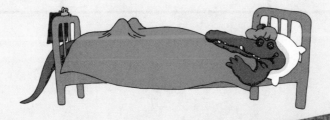

Try This!

On another sheet of paper, list five kinds of pets. Then, add one animal that is not a pet to your list. Ask a friend to read your list and circle the animal that does not belong.

Where to Wear?

Directions: Write each word in the correct column.

head	feet	hands
_____	_____	_____
_____	_____	_____

shoe

ring

hat

cap

glove

sock

Try This!

On another sheet of paper, make a tally chart that shows the different types of shirts in your closet. Sort the shirts by style (short sleeve, long sleeve, etc.) or color.

How Many Legs?

Directions: Cut out the pictures. Glue each picture in the correct column. Draw one more picture in each column.

two legs	four legs	six legs

cut

The Right Name

Directions: Cut and glue the picture of each noun where it belongs.

Person

Place

Thing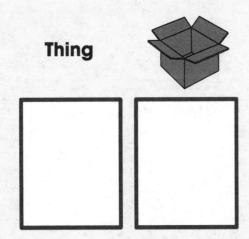

girl | school | firefighter | key | book | farm

cut

Add Some More

Directions: Write **s** or **es** to make each word plural. Choose three words and draw the plural forms.

horse _____

box _____

shoe _____

dish _____

match _____

pumpkin _____

drum _____

table _____

bear _____

Draw pictures to illustrate three plural nouns.
Ask a friend to write the plural word for each of your pictures.

One, Two, or Three

Directions: Circle the correct plural word to complete each sentence.

1. Put the (boxes   boxs) in the garage.

2. The (dishs   dishes) in the sink are dirty.

Directions: Circle the correct word to complete each sentence.

3. The _____ are in a traffic jam.

    car   cars

4. The _____ is pretty tonight.

    moon   moons

On another sheet of paper, list 10 things you see in your home.
Ask a friend to make each word plural.

People on the Go

Directions: Write the verb from the word bank that matches each picture.

cook	drive	sew	swim

 1. _____

 2. _____

 3. _____

 4. _____

Directions: Write the verb from the word bank that completes each sentence.

feeds	plants	works

5. Mr. Henry _____ hard on his farm.

6. He _____ all of the hungry animals.

7. He _____ corn and oats.

Try This!

Look around you. On another sheet of paper, write five sentences about what people are doing. Circle the verb in each sentence.

Baked a Cake

Directions: Write the verb that tells what has already happened.

1. Mom _____ the cake pan.

     washes   washed

2. My brother _____ the cake batter.

            stirred   stirs

3. I _____ the milk.

    poured   pour

Directions: Write the verb to show what already happened.

4. I (help) wash the dishes. _____

 **Try This!**

On another sheet of paper, list five things you do every day.
If you have already done any of those things today, use past-tense verbs to explain.

86

Matt Was the Star

Directions: Write **was** or **were** to complete each sentence.

1. Matt and Rachel _____ excited.

2. The school play _____ about to start.

3. The play _____ about a toy maker.

4. I _____ the toy maker in the play.

Directions: Which linking verb is correct? Write **was** or **were** beside each noun phrase.

5. the stage _____

6. the show _____

7. the toys _____

8. the actors _____

On another sheet of paper, finish the story about Matt and the play.
Circle each linking verb in your story.

Directions: Circle the adjectives.

1. big shoe

2. fuzzy puppy

3. tiny pebble

4. three bears

Directions: Write an adjective to describe each noun.

5. _____ dog

6. _____ bicycle

7. _____ squirrel

8. _____ cowboy

Try This!

On another sheet of paper, draw a picture of yourself. Write five adjectives that describe you or your picture.

The Perfect Start

Directions: Circle the letters that need to be capitalized. Choose one sentence to rewrite on the lines. Remember to use correct capitalization.

1. she played ball on our team.

2. dr. sharma is our dentist.

3. do you know paul brown?

4. we are going to atlanta in december.

5. may we go to the park on sunday?

6. on tuesday, we can go swimming.

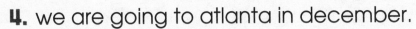

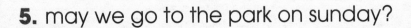

On another sheet of paper, write all of the words on this month's calendar that are capitalized.

89

Fishing for Answers

Directions: Write the first word of each question. Remember to begin with a capital letter. End each question with a question mark. On the last line, write your own question about the picture.

1. _____ that your boat _____
   (is)

2. _____ you catch that fish _____
   (did)

3. _____ much does it weigh _____
   (how)

4. _____ you eat it _____
   (will)

5. _____

Try This!

Interview a friend or a family member. Write five questions you would like to ask. Write the answers under the questions.

For You to Decide

Directions: Write the correct punctuation mark at the end of each sentence. Color the boxes with a question mark red.

I. May I play outside ☐

2. What is your name ☐

3. I am moving next week ☐

4. Math is my favorite subject ☐

5. Can you tie your shoes ☐

6. When do we go home ☐

7. I ate soup for lunch today ☐

8. Can we go to the beach ☐

On another sheet of paper, write three questions.
Remember to use correct punctuation.

Bat Basics

Directions: Write each sentence with a capital letter and end with a period or a question mark.

bats are the only flying mammals

_____

some bats live in caves

_____

i love to read about bats

_____

do all bats eat insects

_____

some bats eat frogs or small fish

_____

 Try This!

On another sheet of paper, write a question about bats. Remember to use correct punctuation. Draw a picture to illustrate your question.

The Picture Tells the Story

Directions: Complete each sentence to match the picture.

1. My friend likes _____.

2. Will you close the _____?

Directions: Complete each sentence. Draw a picture to illustrate each sentence.

3. I want _____.

4. She went _____.

Try This!

Write one sentence that asks a question, one sentence that is a statement, and one sentence that shows excitement. Ask a friend to write the punctuation marks.

Little Acorn Grows Up

Directions: Write **First**, **Next**, and **Last** beside each picture to put them in order. Write about what happens in each picture.

**Try
This!**

On another sheet of paper, draw a picture of a leaf pile and write the steps for raking
leaves in autumn. Use the words **First**, **Next**, and **Last** in your sentences.

94

In the Future

Directions: Draw a picture in the oval of what you want to do when you grow up. Finish the story.

When I grow up, I want to be a

_____

_____

because . . .

_____

_____

_____

_____

_____

_____

_____

_____

What questions do you have about your dream job? Write five of them on another sheet of paper. Ask a family member to help you find the answers.

95

Brothers and Sisters

Directions: Ms. Keith's first-grade class completed a Venn diagram about whether the students have siblings. Use the diagram to answer the questions.

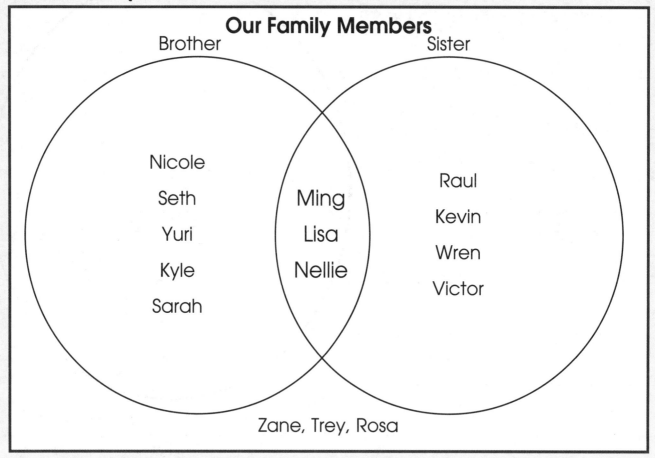

Our Family Members

Brother — Sister

Nicole
Seth
Yuri
Kyle
Sarah

Ming
Lisa
Nellie

Raul
Kevin
Wren
Victor

Zane, Trey, Rosa

1. How many students have a brother? _____

2. How many students have a sister? _____

3. How many students have a brother and a sister? _____

4. How many students have neither a brother nor a sister? _____

5. How many students are in Ms. Keith's class? _____

Try This!

What makes a good brother or sister? List five characteristics of a good sibling.

The Picture Tells the Story

Directions: Complete each sentence to match the picture.

1. My friend likes _____.

2. Will you close the _____?

Directions: Complete each sentence. Draw a picture to illustrate each sentence.

3. I want _____.

4. She went _____.

Write one sentence that asks a question, one sentence that is a statement, and one sentence that shows excitement. Ask a friend to write the punctuation marks.

93

Little Acorn Grows Up

Directions: Write **First**, **Next**, and **Last** beside each picture to put them in order. Write about what happens in each picture.

Try This!

On another sheet of paper, draw a picture of a leaf pile and write the steps for raking leaves in autumn. Use the words **First**, **Next**, and **Last** in your sentences.

94

Anna Is on Time!

Directions: Cut out the sentences. Glue each sentence under the correct picture.

Anna's alarm clock rings.

Anna picks up her books.

Anna is getting hungry.

Anna hears the school bell ring.

cut

It is time to get up.

It is time to go to school.

It is time to go home from school.

It is time to eat lunch.

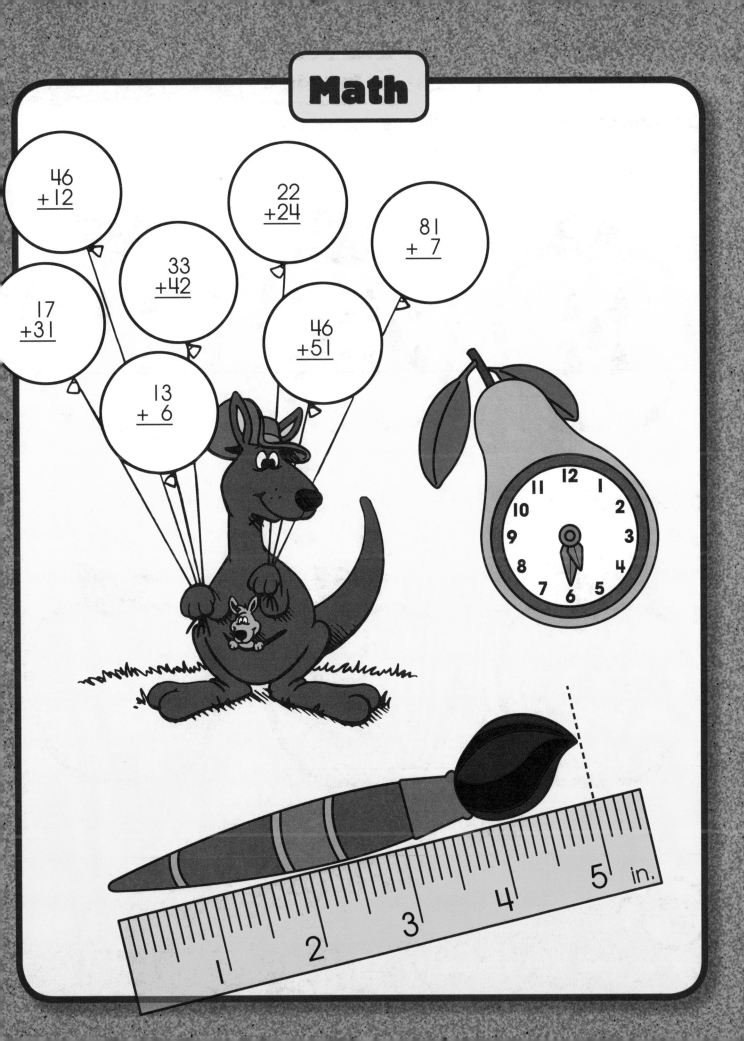

Apple Insides

Directions: Count the seeds in each apple. Write that number on the leaf.

Directions: Draw the correct number of seeds in each apple.

How many seeds are there altogether?

98

Watermelon Garden

Directions: Count the watermelons. Write the number in each watermelon. Circle each group of **10**.

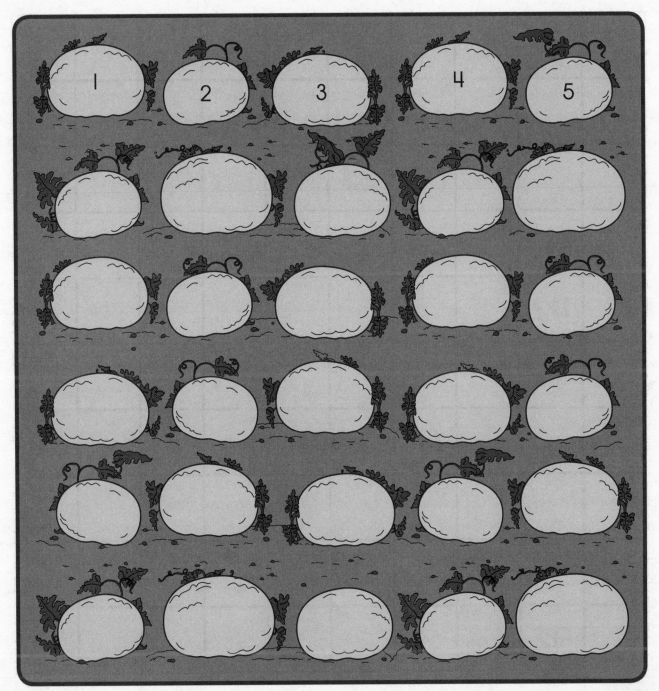

Color odd-numbered watermelons green and even-numbered watermelons yellow.

99

One Hundred Places

Directions: Write the missing numbers. Circle each number that ends with **0**.

		3						
11								
			25					30
			34					
	42							
51								
			64					70
					76			
			85					
	92							

Try This!

Make a number pattern. Color square number 1 blue, square number 2 red, and square number 3 blue to make the ABA pattern.

Take a Step Back

Directions: Count each set of objects. Write the number that comes before.

1. _____

2. _____

3. _____

4. _____

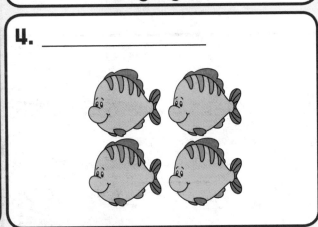

Directions: Draw a set of objects that shows the number that comes before.

3

5

Count backward from 20. Write the numbers on another sheet of paper.

Right in the Middle of Things

Directions: Count each set of objects. Write the number that comes
between.

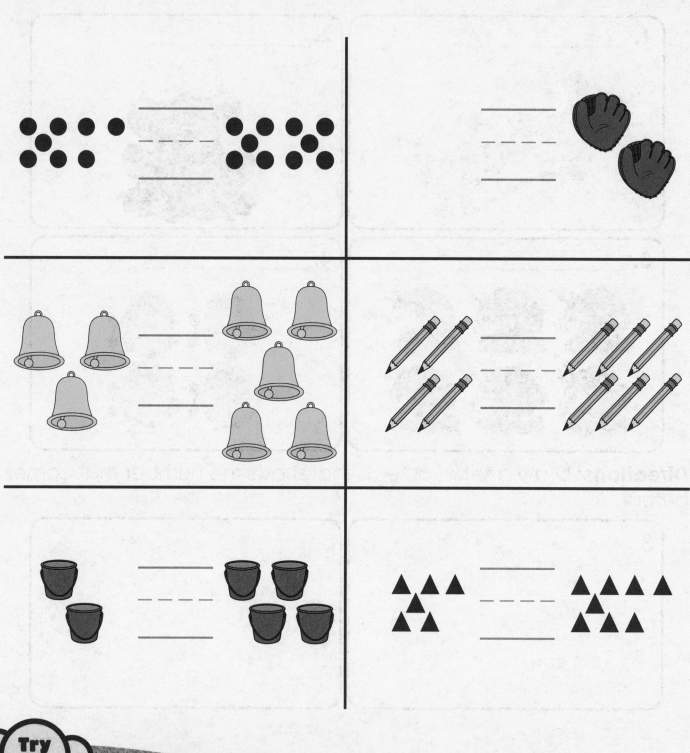

Try This!

What day comes between Friday and Sunday?
On another sheet of paper, write a sentence telling what you like to do on that day.

What Comes Next?

Directions: Count each set of objects. Write the number that comes after.

1. _____

2. _____

3. _____

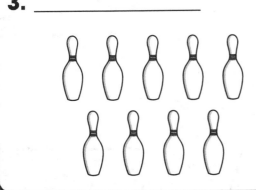

4. _____

Directions: Draw a set of objects that shows the number that comes after.

2

6

Find 10 small objects. Put them in order by size. Then, try putting them into **ABC** order.

A Little Less or a Little More

Directions: Circle the smallest number in each shape. Draw an **X** on the greatest number in each shape.

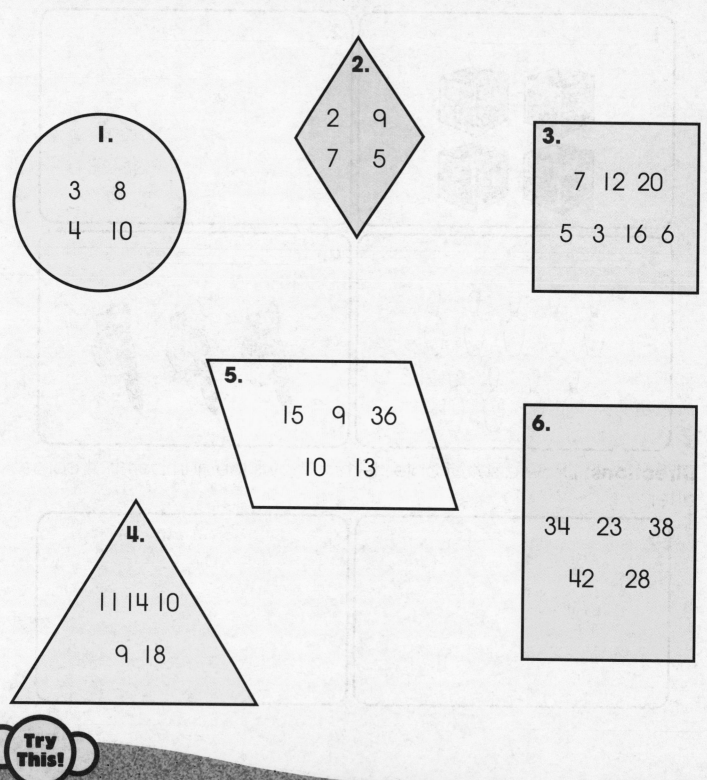

1.
3 8
4 10

2.
2 9
7 5

3.
7 12 20
5 3 16 6

5.
15 9 36
10 13

6.
34 23 38
42 28

4.
11 14 10
9 18

Try This!

On another sheet of paper, write each set of numbers in order from least to greatest.

One Has Fewer

Directions: Circle the amount that is less in each box.

1.

_____

2.

_____

3.

_____

4.

_____

5.

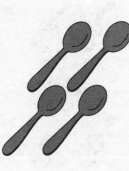   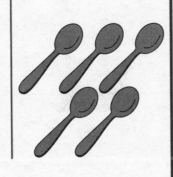

_____

6.

_____

Write > or < on each line to show greater than or less than for each box.

One Has More

Directions: Circle the amount that is more in each box.

1.

___

2.

___

3.

___

4.

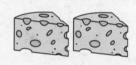 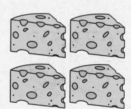

___

5.

___

6.

___

Try This!

Write > or < on each line to show greater than or less than for each box.

Could Be More or Less

Directions: Fill in the number line.

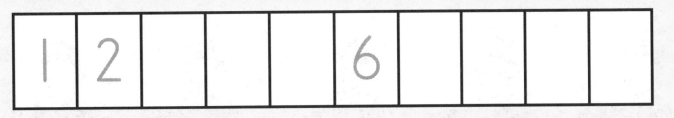

| 1 | 2 | | | | 6 | | | | |

5 > 3

5 is greater than **3**.

3 < 5

3 is less than **5**.

Directions: Write **>** or **<** to show greater than or less than. Use the number line to help you.

I. 5 ____ 2   **2.** 1 ____ 7   **3.** 1 ____ 9   **4.** 8 ____ 5

5. 3 ____ 4   **6.** 9 ____ 3   **7.** 8 ____ 7   **8.** 2 ____ 4

9. 6 ____ 5   **10.** 5 ____ 3   **II.** 5 ____ 7   **12.** 3 ____ 5

Try This!

On another sheet of paper, draw a tree with apples on it. Ask one friend to draw an apple tree that shows fewer apples and another friend to draw a tree that shows more apples.

First in Fire Safety

Directions: Draw lines to match the pictures to the correct order words.

third   **first**   **second**   **fifth**   **fourth**

Directions: Write the order word for each of the fire hydrants.

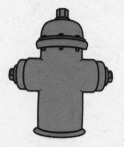   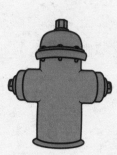 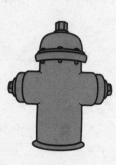

_____   _____   _____   _____   _____

Try This!

Pretend you are in line. Four children are in front of you, and two are behind you.
What position in line are you? Draw a picture to show where you are in line.

108

Leaping Lily Pads!

Directions: Count by **2**s to lead the frog to the log. Color the lily pads that show the number path.

If you could have 50 of something, what would it be? Explain your answer on another sheet of paper.

109

Does the Trash Count?

Directions: Count by **5**s to **50**. Write the numbers on the lines.

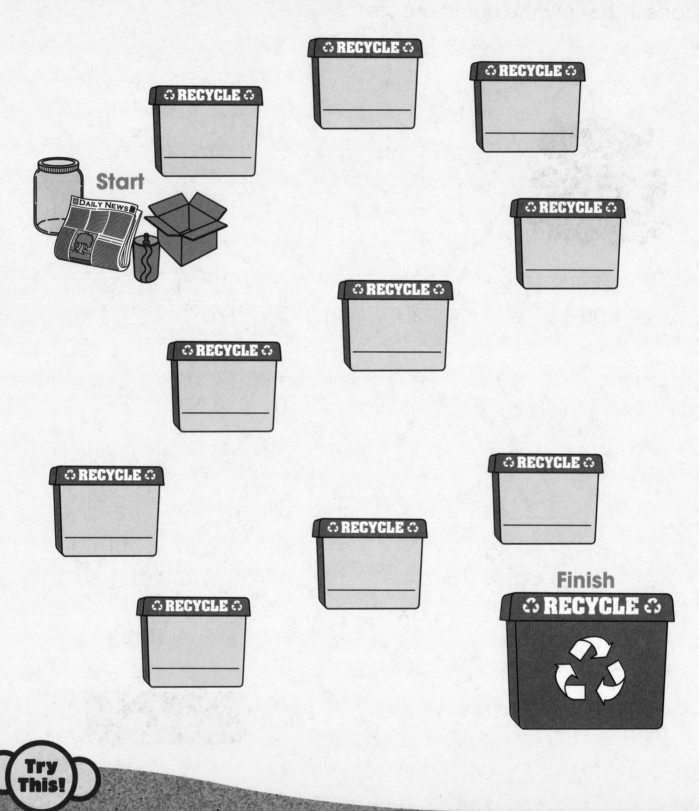

Work with a friend to make a recycling poster.
Draw five things from school and five things from home that can be recycled.

Letters in the Mail

Directions: Cut out the mailboxes. Glue each mailbox on the correct post.

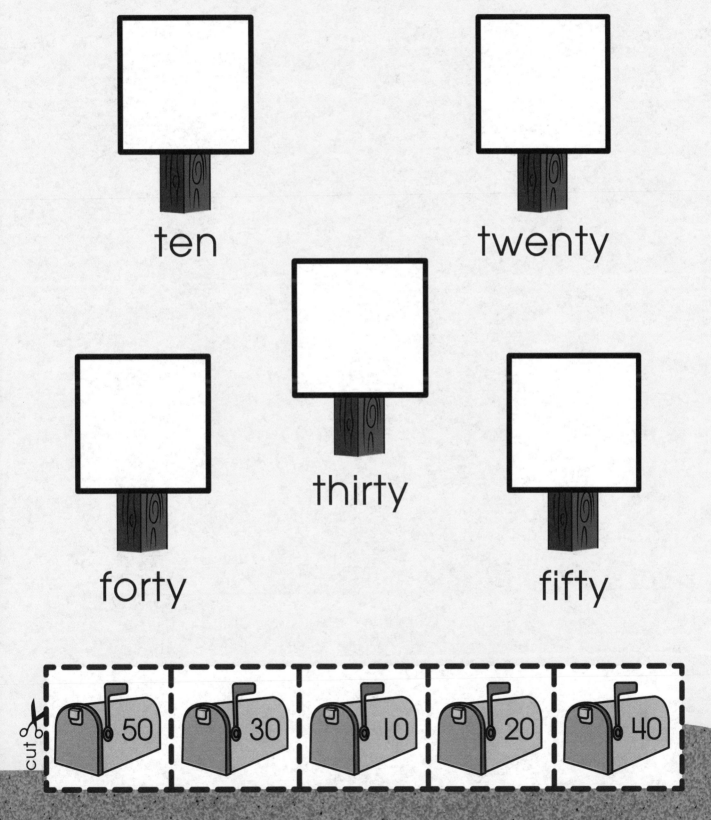

ten

twenty

thirty

forty

fifty

cut

50 30 10 20 40

Half as Much Fun

Directions: Color $\frac{1}{2}$ of each shape or object.

On a separate sheet of paper, draw four new shapes or objects. Color $\frac{1}{2}$ of each shape or object red and $\frac{1}{2}$ of each shape or object blue.

It Shows This Much

Directions: Circle the fraction shown in each picture.

1.

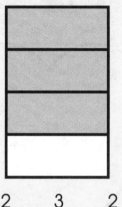

$\frac{1}{3}$ $\frac{1}{4}$ $\frac{1}{2}$

2.

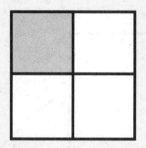

$\frac{1}{3}$ $\frac{1}{4}$ $\frac{2}{4}$

3.

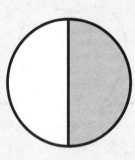

$\frac{2}{3}$ $\frac{3}{4}$ $\frac{2}{4}$

4.

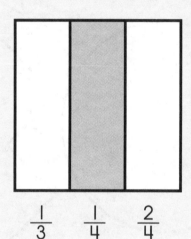

$\frac{1}{3}$ $\frac{1}{4}$ $\frac{2}{4}$

Directions: Color each picture to show the fraction.

5.

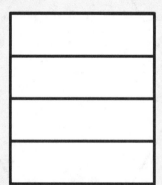

$\frac{2}{4}$

6.

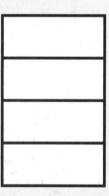

$\frac{1}{4}$

Try This!

Write these fractions in order from least to greatest: $\frac{1}{4}$ $\frac{3}{4}$ $\frac{2}{4}$

Equal Parts Make a Whole

Directions: Write the number of equal parts.

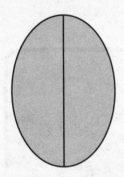

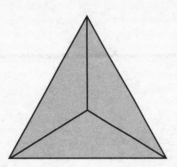

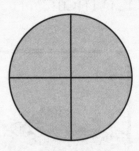

_____

_____

_____

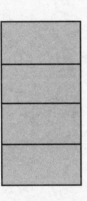

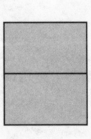

_____

_____

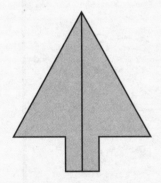

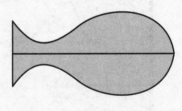

_____

_____

_____

Cut a square out of construction paper. Fold it into four equal parts. Label each part with the correct function.

Sums of Shells

Directions: Add. Write the sums. Go through the tunnels to connect each matching sum.

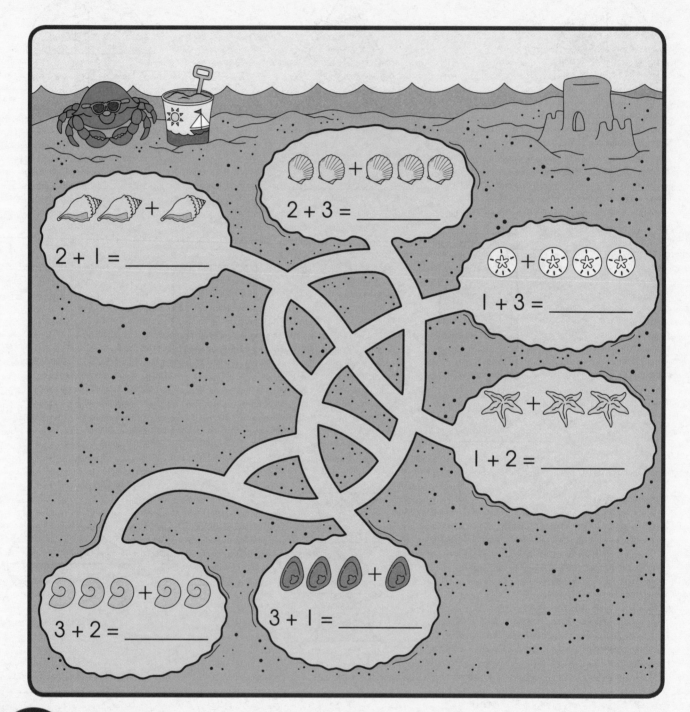

2 + 1 = _____

2 + 3 = _____

1 + 3 = _____

1 + 2 = _____

3 + 2 = _____

3 + 1 = _____

 **Try This!**

On another sheet of paper, write five addition problems that all have a sum of 10.

Under-the-Sea Addition

Directions: Solve the problems. Use the code to color the picture.

0 and 1 = yellow
4 and 5 = orange

2 and 3 = blue
6 and 7 = purple

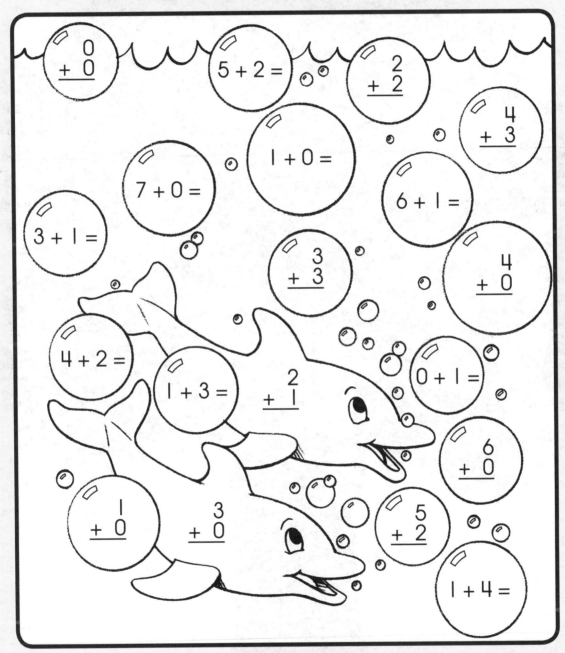

$$\begin{array}{r} 0 \\ + 0 \\ \hline \end{array}$$

5 + 2 =

$$\begin{array}{r} 2 \\ + 2 \\ \hline \end{array}$$

$$\begin{array}{r} 4 \\ + 3 \\ \hline \end{array}$$

1 + 0 =

7 + 0 =

6 + 1 =

3 + 1 =

$$\begin{array}{r} 3 \\ + 3 \\ \hline \end{array}$$

$$\begin{array}{r} 4 \\ + 0 \\ \hline \end{array}$$

4 + 2 =

1 + 3 =

$$\begin{array}{r} 2 \\ + 1 \\ \hline \end{array}$$

0 + 1 =

$$\begin{array}{r} 6 \\ + 0 \\ \hline \end{array}$$

$$\begin{array}{r} 1 \\ + 0 \\ \hline \end{array}$$

$$\begin{array}{r} 3 \\ + 0 \\ \hline \end{array}$$

$$\begin{array}{r} 5 \\ + 2 \\ \hline \end{array}$$

1 + 4 =

On another sheet of paper, write an addition word problem about the dolphins in the picture. Write the matching number sentence under the problem.

Apples in All

Directions: Solve the problems. Draw a line to match each problem to the correct answer.

8 + 2   15
9 + 6   4
2 + 2   10

1 + 2   11
6 + 7   3
5 + 6   13

6 + 6   12
6 + 3   9
3 + 4   7

3 + 2   10
6 + 8   14
5 + 5   5

6 + 2   8
1 + 1   6
1 + 5   2

Try This!

Do more of your friends like red or green apples?
Ask seven friends their favorite flavors and write an addition sentence using the numbers.

Add All Three

Directions: Solve the problems. Write the sums in order from least to greatest on the lines below.

7 4 + 2	6 5 + 3	4 4 + 3	4 3 + 6
☐	☐	☐	☐

4 2 + 5	4 6 + 2	7 2 + 4	8 8 + 1
☐	☐	☐	☐

_____ _____ _____ _____ _____ _____ _____ _____

On another sheet of paper, write two addition problems that each have three addends and a sum of 12.

119

Double-Digit Sums

Directions: Solve the problems. Color the spaces with sums greater than 50 red. Color the spaces with sums less than 50 blue.

 **Try This!**

Draw two empty balloons. Inside the balloons, write one addition problem that has a sum greater than 50 and one that has a sum less than 50. Color the balloons the correct color.

Presidential Addition

Directions: Solve the problems. Use the answers to solve the riddle.

N	**A**	**O**	**S**
14 +17	26 +47	35 +25	17 +29

T	**H**	**B**	**E**
16 +36	53 +18	19 +21	29 +29

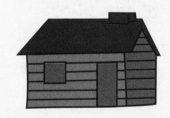

What is a nickname for the 16th president of the United States?

$$\overline{71} \ \overline{60} \ \overline{31} \ \overline{58} \ \overline{46} \ \overline{52} \qquad \overline{73} \ \overline{40} \ \overline{58}$$

With an adult, use the Internet to find a picture of the 16th U.S. president. Write three facts and three opinions about this president.

Solving Problems in the Stars

Directions: Subtract. Write the differences. Color each space with a difference of 2 or 3 yellow. Color the rest of the spaces purple.

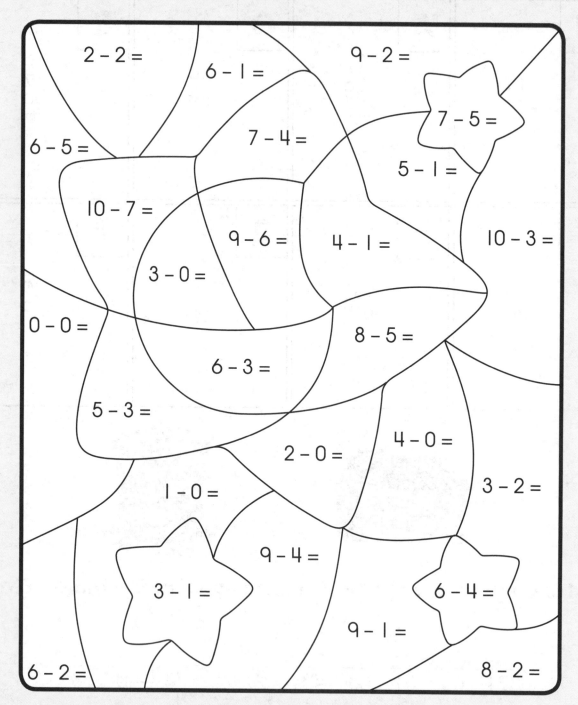

2 − 2 =

6 − 1 =

9 − 2 =

6 − 5 =

7 − 4 =

7 − 5 =

5 − 1 =

10 − 7 =

9 − 6 =

4 − 1 =

10 − 3 =

3 − 0 =

0 − 0 =

8 − 5 =

6 − 3 =

5 − 3 =

4 − 0 =

2 − 0 =

3 − 2 =

1 − 0 =

9 − 4 =

3 − 1 =

6 − 4 =

9 − 1 =

6 − 2 =

8 − 2 =

Try This!

Jay saw 9 shooting stars. He made wishes on 6 of them. How many stars did he not wish on? Write a subtraction sentence that shows the problem. Then, find the answer.

Springtime Subtraction

Directions: Subtract. Use the code to color the worms.

1 = red	3 = yellow
2 = orange	4 = brown

 5 – 1 =

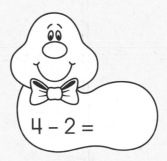 4 – 2 =

 5 – 2 =

 3 – 1 =

 4 – 3 =

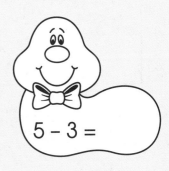 5 – 3 =

 2 – 1 =

 4 – 1 =

 3 – 2 =

 **Try This!**

A total of 8 birds were in a tree. Some flew away, and 3 birds were left. How many birds flew away? Write a subtraction sentence that shows the problem. Then, find the answer.

Exploring Differences

Directions: Solve the problems. Use the answers to solve the riddle.

P

19
- 4

T

14
- 2

I

5
- 1

N

9
- 6

M

9
- 0

A

15
- 4

S

19
- 1

R

7
- 0

What three "friends" did Columbus sail with?

___ ___ ___ ___ , ___ ___ ___ ___ ___ ___ , and
3   4   3   11   15   4   3   12   11

___ ___ ___ ___ ___   ___ ___ ___ ___ ___ .
18   11   3   12   11   9   11   7   4   11

Try This!

If you could explore a new land, where would it be, and how would you get there?
Explain your answer on another sheet of paper.

Bees and Flower Favorites

Directions: Subtract the numbers to find the differences. Cut out
and glue the differences next to the flowers.

$$\begin{array}{r} 54 \\ -22 \\ \hline \end{array}$$

$$\begin{array}{r} 62 \\ -10 \\ \hline \end{array}$$

$$\begin{array}{r} 27 \\ -14 \\ \hline \end{array}$$

$$\begin{array}{r} 41 \\ -20 \\ \hline \end{array}$$

$$\begin{array}{r} 62 \\ -21 \\ \hline \end{array}$$

$$\begin{array}{r} 39 \\ -17 \\ \hline \end{array}$$

$$\begin{array}{r} 75 \\ -52 \\ \hline \end{array}$$

$$\begin{array}{r} 81 \\ -20 \\ \hline \end{array}$$

$$\begin{array}{r} 90 \\ -80 \\ \hline \end{array}$$

32	52	21
41	23	61
13	22	10

cut

Try This!

On a separate sheet of paper, draw a picture of your favorite flower.
Label the parts of the flower.

Lucky in Subtraction

Directions: Subtract. Cut out and glue the pot of gold with the matching answer on each rainbow.

$$\begin{array}{r} 71 \\ -19 \\ \hline \end{array}$$

$$\begin{array}{r} 23 \\ -14 \\ \hline \end{array}$$

$$\begin{array}{r} 75 \\ -39 \\ \hline \end{array}$$

$$\begin{array}{r} 62 \\ -27 \\ \hline \end{array}$$

$$\begin{array}{r} 55 \\ -36 \\ \hline \end{array}$$

$$\begin{array}{r} 46 \\ -28 \\ \hline \end{array}$$

cut

9   35   52   19   36   18

Bananas over Math

Directions: Write **+** or **−** to make each problem correct. Trace a path to connect each monkey to the correct banana. For Marcus, connect all of the addition problems. For Mona, connect all of the subtraction problems.

Marcus

Mona

3 ◯ 2 = 5

3 ◯ 3 = 0

5 ◯ 5 = 10

9 ◯ 1 = 10

9 ◯ 4 = 5

2 ◯ 6 = 8

10 ◯ 8 = 2

5 ◯ 4 = 9

10 ◯ 3 = 7

6 ◯ 4 = 10

8 ◯ 2 = 6

5 ◯ 2 = 7

7 ◯ 3 = 4

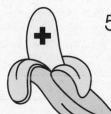

5 ◯ 3 = 8

6 ◯ 3 = 3

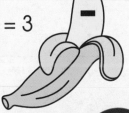

2 ◯ 7 = 9

Try
This!

What animals live in a rain forest? On another sheet of paper, draw a picture of a rain forest that shows at least five animals. Write three sentences telling about your picture.

Magnet Math

Directions: Solve the problems. Use the answers to solve the riddle.

N	T	H	R	P	L
$\begin{array}{r} 5 \\ +\ 5 \\ \hline \end{array}$	$\begin{array}{r} 14 \\ -\ 12 \\ \hline \end{array}$	$\begin{array}{r} 19 \\ -\ 6 \\ \hline \end{array}$	$\begin{array}{r} 4 \\ +\ 7 \\ \hline \end{array}$	$\begin{array}{r} 3 \\ +\ 1 \\ \hline \end{array}$	$\begin{array}{r} 15 \\ +\ 4 \\ \hline \end{array}$

O	E	S	U	A	D
$\begin{array}{r} 7 \\ -\ 2 \\ \hline \end{array}$	$\begin{array}{r} 7 \\ +\ 8 \\ \hline \end{array}$	$\begin{array}{r} 12 \\ -\ 6 \\ \hline \end{array}$	$\begin{array}{r} 10 \\ -\ 7 \\ \hline \end{array}$	$\begin{array}{r} 17 \\ -\ 9 \\ \hline \end{array}$	$\begin{array}{r} 9 \\ +\ 8 \\ \hline \end{array}$

What do magnets have in common with the earth?

Answer: They both have . . .

$\underline{\quad}$ $\underline{\quad}$ $\underline{\quad}$ $\underline{\quad}$ $\underline{\quad}$ $\underline{\quad}$
  8   10   5   11   2   13

$\underline{\quad}$ $\underline{\quad}$ $\underline{\quad}$ $\underline{\quad}$ $\underline{\quad}$ $\underline{\quad}$ $\underline{\quad}$ $\underline{\quad}$
  4   5   19   15   8   10   17   8

$\underline{\quad}$ $\underline{\quad}$ $\underline{\quad}$ $\underline{\quad}$ $\underline{\quad}$ $\underline{\quad}$ $\underline{\quad}$ $\underline{\quad}$ $\underline{\quad}$.
  6   5   3   2   13   4   5   19   15

Try This!

On another sheet of paper, list five things that are attracted to magnets and five things that are not attracted to magnets.

Staying Healthy

Directions: Solve the problems. Circle the healthful foods. Draw a box around each food that you should only eat once in a while.

$$\begin{array}{r} 14 \\ + 11 \\ \hline \end{array}$$

$$\begin{array}{r} 72 \\ - 51 \\ \hline \end{array}$$

$$\begin{array}{r} 8 \\ - 5 \\ \hline \end{array}$$

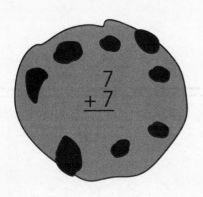

$$\begin{array}{r} 7 \\ + 7 \\ \hline \end{array}$$

$$\begin{array}{r} 38 \\ + 21 \\ \hline \end{array}$$

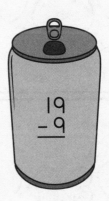

$$\begin{array}{r} 19 \\ - 9 \\ \hline \end{array}$$

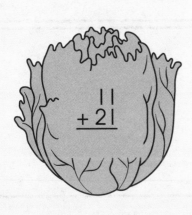

$$\begin{array}{r} 11 \\ + 21 \\ \hline \end{array}$$

$$\begin{array}{r} 9 \\ - 3 \\ \hline \end{array}$$

$$\begin{array}{r} 14 \\ + 13 \\ \hline \end{array}$$

Try This!

On another sheet of paper, write or draw a shopping list for 10 healthful snacks.

Hearts in a Row

Directions: Continue the patterns. Color the large hearts red and the small hearts pink.

Try This!

Draw hearts on a sentence strip. Color the hearts to show a pattern.
Tape the sentence strip together to make a hat.

132

Berries in Baskets

Directions: Draw the correct number of strawberries in the baskets to continue each pattern.

1.

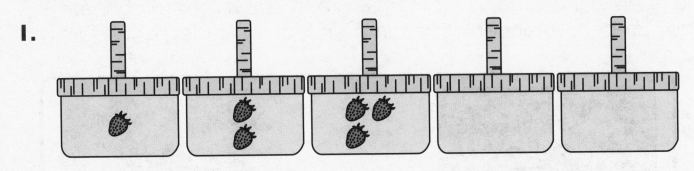

2.

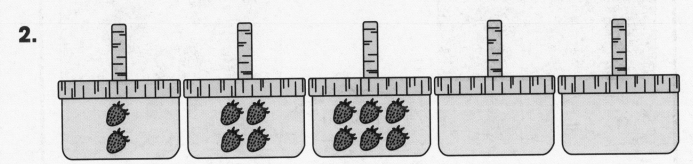

3.

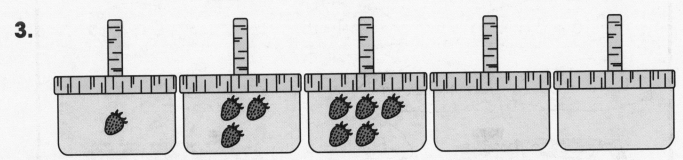

Directions: Make your own pattern.

4.

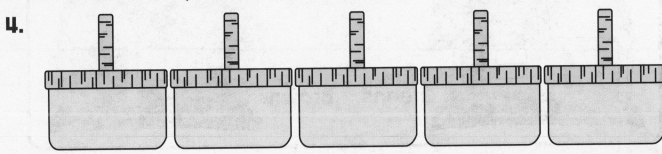

What grows on a farm besides strawberries? On another sheet of paper, draw a picture of a farm that includes at least five types of crops. Label the crops.

Fact Family Fun

Directions: Color the number sentences that show numbers in the Brown's fact family brown. Color the number sentences that show numbers in the Green's fact family green. Draw lines to connect the number sentences in the same fact family to lead each family home.

The Greens

6
9
3

The Browns

9
12
3

9 – 6 = 3

9 + 3 = 12

3 + 6 = 9

12 – 9 = 3

6 + 3 = 9

4 + 4 = 8

3 + 9 = 12

9 – 3 = 6

1 + 9 = 10

12 – 3 = 9

5 + 1 = 6

9
3
6
The Greens

12
3
9
The Browns

Try This!

On another sheet of paper, draw your own fact family house. Write the three numbers in the fact family on the roof. Write the addition and subtraction number sentences in the house.

Food Rules!

Directions: Write each word from the word bank in the correct food group.

milk

_____
_____
_____
_____

meats & beans

_____
_____
_____
_____

bagel
beans
butter
carrots
cheese
cherries
chicken
cottage cheese
fish
ham
lettuce
olive oil
oranges
pears
rolls
toast
yogurt

fruits

_____
_____
_____
_____

oils

_____
_____
_____
_____

vegetables

_____
_____
_____
_____

grains

_____
_____
_____
_____

On another sheet of paper, sort the same foods by another rule. Explain your sorting rule.

Hats Off to Math

Directions: Draw the missing pictures. Finish the number sentences.

1.

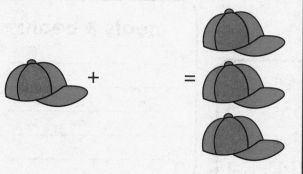 + =

1 + _____ = 3

2.

 + =

3 + _____ = 5

3.

 + =

5 + _____ = 8

4.

 + =

3 + _____ = 6

5.

 + =

2 + _____ = 7

6.

 + =

4 + _____ = 5

 **Try This!**

Above each problem, rewrite the addition sentence as a subtraction sentence.

136

Happy About Math

Directions: Draw the missing pictures. Finish the number sentences.

1.

3 – _____ = 1

2.

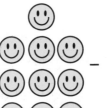

10 – _____ = 7

3.

12 – _____ = 6

4.

8 – _____ = 7

Directions: Make up your own problem.

_____ =

Above each problem, rewrite the subtraction sentence as an addition sentence.

137

Something Is Missing!

Directions: Write the missing number to complete each number sentence.

6 + ☐ = 12   7 + ☐ = 12

```
  13
- ☐
————
   4
```

20 − ☐ = 1   11 − ☐ = 2

```
   5
+ ☐
————
  13
```

15 − ☐ = 1   8 + ☐ = 11

```
   3
+ ☐
————
  13
```

7 + ☐ = 14   12 − ☐ = 3

```
  18
- ☐
————
   9
```

Try This!

Make up two of your own problems.   ☐ + ☐ = 12   ☐ + ☐ = 10

Horses in Corrals

Directions: Cut out the horses. Glue each horse on the correct corral.

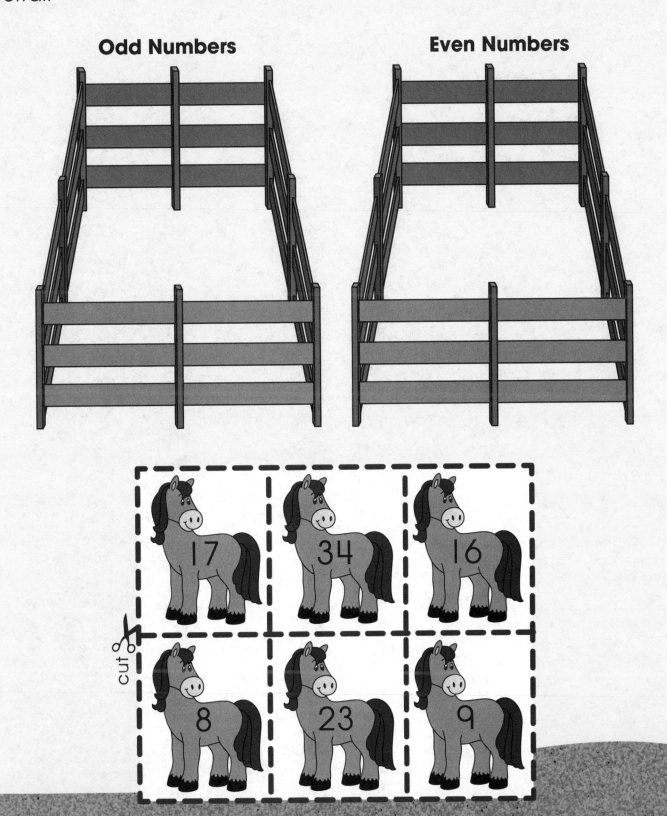

Odd Numbers

Even Numbers

cut

17   34   16

8   23   9

Tens and Ones

Directions: Write the number of objects in each set.

_____

_____

_____

_____

_____

_____

_____

_____

Directions: Write the value of each number.

29 = _____ tens and _____ ones

34 = _____ tens and _____ ones

18 = _____ ten and _____ ones

48 = _____ tens and _____ ones

Try This!

On another sheet of paper, draw a picture that shows 3 tens and 4 ones.

Building Three-Digit Numbers

Directions: Write how many hundreds, tens, and ones are in each number.

152 = _____ tens _____ hundred _____ ones

347 = _____ hundreds _____ tens _____ ones

201 = _____ tens _____ hundreds _____ one

136 = _____ ones _____ tens _____ hundred

463 = _____ hundreds _____ ones _____ tens

Try This!

Round each number above to the nearest hundred.

More Than One Way

Directions: Draw lines to match the equal numbers.

49 •

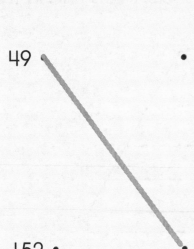

• • 4 tens
9 ones

152 •

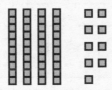

• • 1 hundred
5 tens
2 ones

355 •

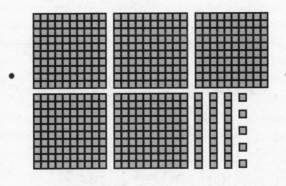

• • 3 hundreds
5 tens
5 ones

535 •

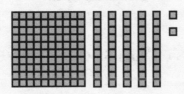

• • 5 hundreds
3 tens
5 ones

On another sheet of paper, write one number three different ways.

Directions: Abraham Lincoln was born in a log cabin. Look at the picture of a log cabin. How many of each shape can you find in the picture?

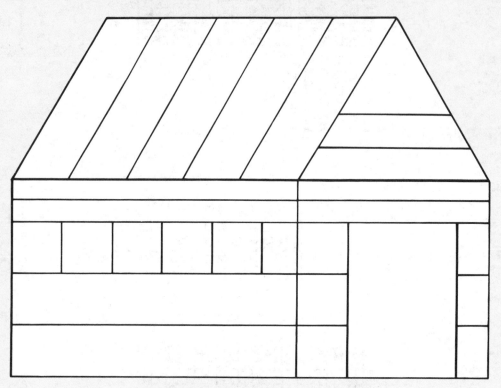

How many △ ? _____ How many ▱ ? _____ How many ☐ ? _____

Draw and color a door.

How many sides does each shape have?

△ _____   ▱ _____   ☐ _____

How many corners does each shape have?

△ _____   ▱ _____   ☐ _____

Try This!

Work with a friend to create a poster about Abraham Lincoln.
Write five facts about Lincoln as a child and five facts about him as an adult.

Practice in 3-D

Directions: Use the code to color the figures.

= red   = green   = blue   = orange

1. How many ⬭ ? _____

2. How many △ ? _____

3. How many ▱ ? _____

4. How many ⬭ ? _____

Try This!

Label each picture as **cone**, **cube**, **sphere**, or **cylinder**.

A Perfect Line?

Directions: Write **yes** or **no** to tell if a line of symmetry is shown.

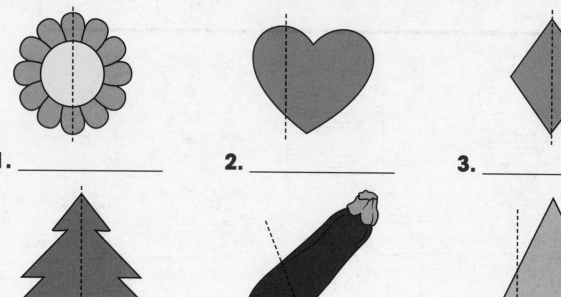

1. _____

2. _____

3. _____

4. _____

5. _____

6. _____

Directions: Draw a line through each object to show two parts that are exactly alike.

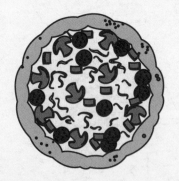

On another sheet of paper, draw five shapes that do not have lines of symmetry.

146

These Seven Days

Directions: Read the paragraph. Answer the questions.

Seven days are in a week. Saturday and Sunday are the weekend days. You go to school the other five days. Which day do you like best?

How many days are in a week?

6   7   10

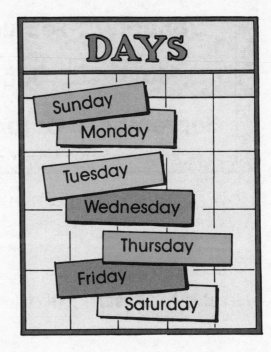

Which two days make a weekend?

_____   _____

Saturday
Thursday
Sunday

Write the five days you go to school.

_____   _____   _____

_____   _____

On another sheet of paper, draw and color what you do on a weekend.
Write three sentences to describe your picture.

147

This Month or Next Month

Directions: Read the paragraph. Answer the questions.

> Twelve months are in a year. The first month is January. The last month is December. Some months have 31 days. Some months have 30 days. February is the shortest month. It has 28 days. Can you name the months of the year?

January	**February**	**March**	**April**
May	**June**	**July**	**August**
September	**October**	**November**	**December**

How many months are in a year?   five   nine   twelve

What is the first month of the year? _____

What is the last month of the year? _____

Some months have 30 days.   YES   NO

Some months have 31 days.   YES   NO

February is the longest month.   YES   NO

February has 28 days.   YES   NO

Try This!

Write your favorite month of the year.
Draw pictures of activities that you like to do during that month.

Seasons of Fun

Directions: Write the season that matches each picture. Cut out the pictures. On a separate sheet of paper, glue the pictures in the correct order. Circle your favorite season.

The season is _____.

The season is _____.

The season is _____.

The season is _____.

On another sheet of paper, write three things that you like to do in your favorite season.

Calendar Exploration

Directions: Trace the number **1**. Write the numbers **2** to **30** to complete the calendar. Answer the questions.

June

Sunday	Monday	Tuesday	Wednesday	Thursday	Friday	Saturday
			1			

1. On what day of the week does June end? _____

2. How many Tuesdays are in June? _____

3. How many Saturdays are in June? _____

Try This!

What other things can a calendar show?
List as many things as you can think of on another sheet of paper.

At This Time Today

Directions: Look at each picture. Write the word from the word bank that tells when the action in the picture happens. Write the numbers **1** to **4** to show the order that the actions happen.

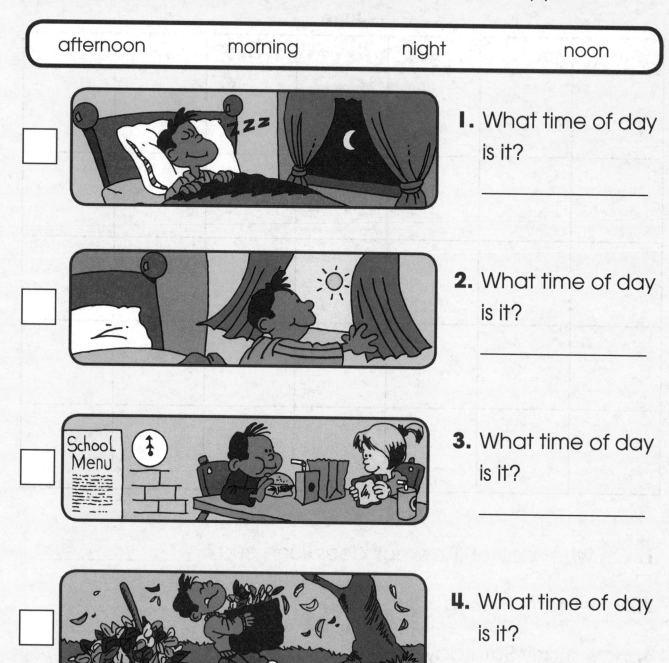

afternoon   morning   night   noon

1. What time of day is it?

   _____

2. What time of day is it?

   _____

3. What time of day is it?

   _____

4. What time of day is it?

   _____

On another sheet of paper, write or draw what you do each day in the morning, at noon, in the afternoon, and at night.

Don't Be Late!

Directions: Draw the clock hands to show the time.

1.

2:00

2.

11:00

3.

4:00

4.

6:00

5.

7:00

6.

9:00

Try This!

What is the difference between A.M. and P.M.? On another sheet of paper, write your answer and list five things you do in the A.M. and five things you do in the P.M.

Time for the Harvest

Directions: Write the time shown on each clock.

_____   _____   _____

_____   _____   _____

Try This!

On another sheet of paper, sort the above foods into lists of fruits and vegetables.
Add five more foods to each list.

Toothy Measures

Directions: Count how many cubes long each object is. Write the number. Circle the things you use to take care of your teeth.

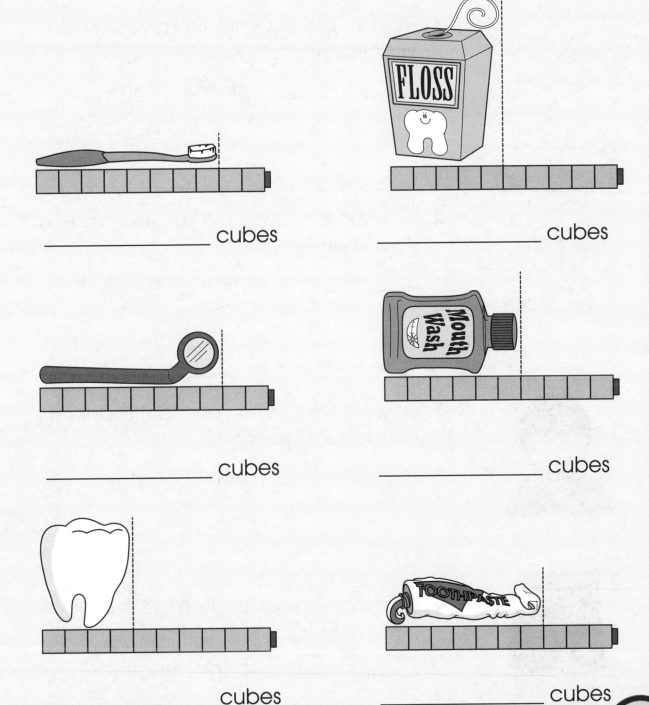

_____ cubes

_____ cubes

_____ cubes

_____ cubes

_____ cubes

_____ cubes

Try This!

How do you take care of your teeth? Explain your answer on another sheet of paper.

The Measure of Me

Directions: Use a pencil to measure different parts of your body.

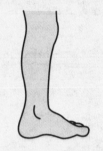

1. How long is your arm from your wrist to your elbow?

_____ pencil lengths

2. How long is your leg from your ankle to your knee?

_____ pencil lengths

3. How long is it from your right shoulder to your left shoulder?

_____ pencil lengths

4. How long is your leg from your knee to your hip?

_____ pencil lengths

Measure five things in your bedroom with your pencil.
On another sheet of paper, record the length of each object.

Measurement Rules!

Directions: Look at each ruler. Write the length of each object. Read the units carefully.

_____ inch

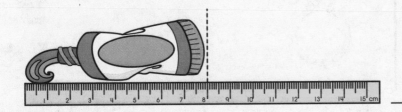

_____ centimeters

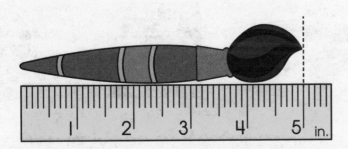

_____ inches

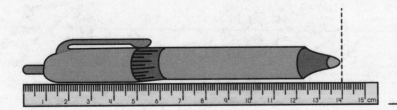

_____ centimeters

Try This!

Use a ruler to measure five objects. On another sheet of paper, write the name of each object and its length in both inches and centimeters.

157

Heavy or Not?

1. Which object weighs less than the object on the scale?

2. Which object weighs more than the toy on the scale?

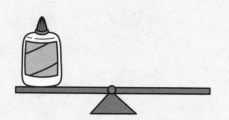  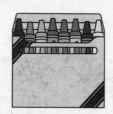 

3. Which object weighs about the same as the object on the scale?

Directions: Number the objects from lightest to heaviest. Write **1** for the lightest object. Write **3** for the heaviest object.

_____   _____   _____

On another sheet of paper, list five things that weigh more than you and five things that weigh less than you.

Rain Forest Riches

Directions: Use the picture to answer the questions.

1. What is the value of all of the quarters? _____

2. What is the value of all of the nickels? _____

3. What is the value of all of the dimes? _____

4. What is the value of all of the pennies? _____

Try This!

Make a rain forest information poster.
Draw five different kinds of animals that live in the rain forest and write three rain forest facts.

Time to Shop

Directions: Look at each box. Circle the item you can buy with the money.

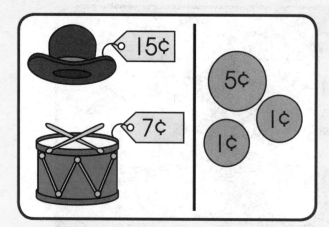

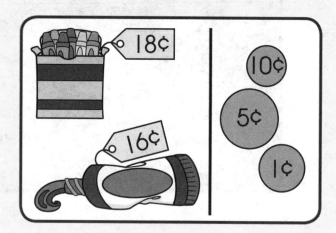

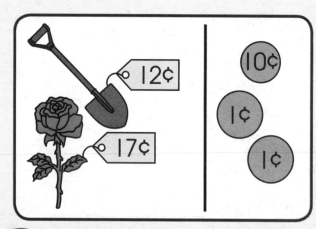

 **Try This!**

If you had 50¢, what three things above would you buy? How much would that cost? How much change would you get back?

Vacation Reading

Directions: The Perez family read during their vacation. Use the graph to answer the questions.

Books Read on Vacation

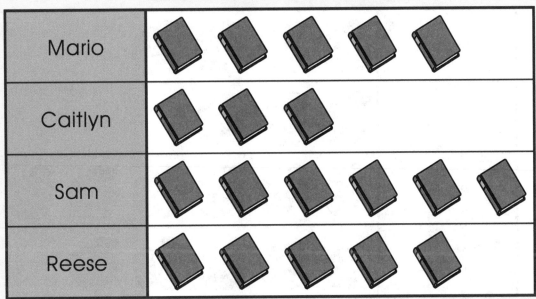

 = 1 book

1. Who read 6 books while on vacation? _____

2. Who read the least number of books? _____

3. How many books did Mario read? _____

4. How many books did Sam and Reese read altogether? _____

5. How many more books did Sam read than Reese? _____

6. How many books did the family read altogether? _____

On another sheet of paper, draw the cover of your favorite book. Write the title on the cover and write four or five sentences about your favorite part.

161

Apple Orchard Trip

Directions: Mr. Kim's first-grade class went to the apple orchard. Use the graph to answer the questions.

Apple Picking

= 5 apples

1. Who picked 30 apples? _____

2. How many apples did Adam pick? _____

3. Who picked the most apples? _____

4. How many more apples did Maria pick than Adam? _____

5. How many apples did Maria and Marcus pick altogether? _____

6. How many apples did the class pick altogether? _____

If each apple tree had 15 apples picked from it, how many trees did Mr. Kim's class pick apples from?

How We Travel

Directions: Mr. Jacob's class made a graph about how they traveled on vacation. Use the graph to answer the questions.

How We Travel on Vacation

	Airplane	Car	Train	Boat
7				
6				
5				
4				
3				
2				
1				
0				

1. How many students traveled by train? _____

2. How did most students travel on vacation? _____

3. What kind of travel was used the least? _____

4. How many more students traveled by car than by airplane? _____

5. How many students traveled by airplane and train combined? _____

Try This!

If you could travel anywhere, where would you go and how would you get there?
Answer the question in three sentences on another sheet of paper.

Pet Tally

Directions: Ms. Smith's first-grade class worked together to complete a tally chart about their pets. Each student made only one tally. Use the chart to answer the questions.

My Pet

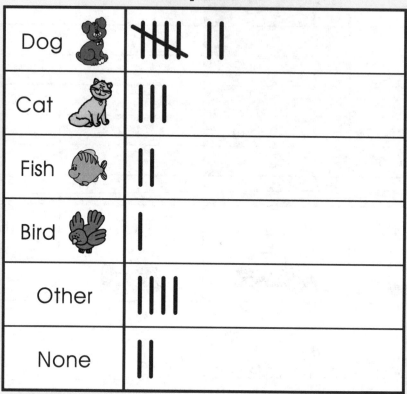

1. How many students have a dog? _____

2. Only one student has a pet _____.

3. How many more students have a dog than a cat? _____

4. How many students do not have a pet? _____

5. How many students are in Ms. Smith's class? _____

 **Try This!**

On another sheet of paper, draw a picture of your pet or a pet you would like to have. Write three sentences about what makes your pet special.

Spin the Spinner!

Directions: Color the spinner. Answer the questions.

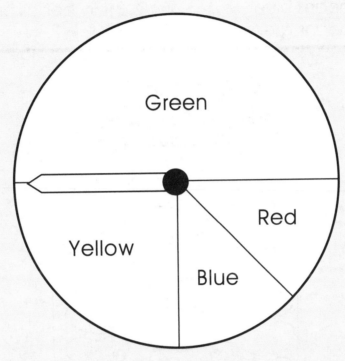

1. What color will the spinner probably land on the most often?

_____

2. What color will the spinner probably land on the least often?

_____

3. Will the spinner be more likely to land on red or yellow?

_____

4. Will the spinner be more likely to land on blue or green?

_____

Create a spinner. Color your spinner to match the one above. Spin the arrow 10 times. Record how often the spinner lands on each color.

Jelly Bean Probability

Directions: Color the jelly beans. Answer the questions.

4 jelly beans red	2 jelly beans yellow
3 jelly beans blue	6 jelly beans orange
5 jelly beans green	

1. If you were to pick without looking, are you more likely to pick a green or yellow jelly bean? _____

2. If you were to pick without looking, what color of jelly bean are you most likely to pick? _____

3. If you were to pick without looking, what color of jelly bean are you least likely to pick? _____

On another sheet of paper, write the probability of picking each color.

Tasty Problems

Directions: Draw pictures to help you solve the problems. Write **healthy** under each box that shows healthful food choices.

1. Claire ate 1 banana and 7 grapes for breakfast. How many pieces of fruit did she eat in all?

_____ pieces of fruit

_____

2. Jay ate 4 pieces of cake last week and 4 pieces of cake this week. How much cake did he eat in all?

_____ pieces of cake

_____

3. Amad ate 2 vegetable servings on Tuesday and 5 vegetable servings on Wednesday. How many vegetable servings did Amad eat altogether?

vegetable servings

_____

4. Ella drank 8 glasses of water yesterday and 8 glasses of water today. How much water did she drink in all?

glasses of water

_____

How many fruits and vegetables do you eat in a day? On another sheet of paper, list the fruits and vegetables you ate yesterday. Write your own word problem about the list.

Pictures and Numbers

Directions: Solve the problems. Show your work with numbers or pictures.

1. Kayla's family went on a road trip. They drove 54 miles on Friday and 25 miles on Saturday. How far did they drive?

_____ miles

2. Nick read 48 pages last week and 51 pages this week. How many pages did he read altogether?

_____ pages

3. Kayla saw 24 ducks and 32 turtles at the lake. How many animals did she see in all?

_____ animals

4. Aiden went on vacation. He took 36 pictures and bought 12 picture postcards. How many pictures does he have in all?

_____ pictures

Try This!

On another sheet of paper, write four word problems.
Ask a friend to solve the problems.

Seasonal Subtraction

Directions: Draw pictures to help you solve the problems. Write the name of each season being described.

1. Greg made 10 snowballs. He gave 5 of them to his sister. How many snowballs does he have left?

_____ snowballs

Season: _____

2. Holly made 7 sand castles while on vacation at the beach. The ocean washed away 4 of them. How many sand castles are left?

_____ sand castles

Season: _____

3. Leo raked 12 piles of leaves. His sister put 8 of the piles in bags. How many piles of leaves are left?

_____ piles of leaves

Season: _____

4. Malia picked 8 flowers. She gave 6 of them to her mom. How many flowers does Malia have left?

_____ flowers

Season: _____

Try This!

On another sheet of paper, write the seasons in order. Write your favorite thing to do in each season.

A Sea of Subtraction

Directions: Solve the problems. Show your work.

1. We saw 26 dolphins playing in the water.
We saw 13 swim away.
How many dolphins are left?

2. There were 48 fish in the coral.
Then, 12 swam away.
How many fish are left?

3. I watched 24 sharks race in the water.
I watched 12 stop to watch fish.
How many sharks are still racing?

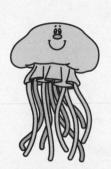

4. A total of 86 jellyfish swam around a sunken ship. A group of 42 swam into the ship. How many jellyfish are still swimming around the ship?

Make an ocean information poster. Draw five or more animals that live in the ocean and write three reasons why the oceans are important.

Working in Gardens

Directions: Read each problem. Decide if you need to add or subtract to find the answer. Solve the problem.

1. Cameron saw 6 birds in the garden. He saw 3 fly away. How many birds are left?

_____ birds

2. Larissa planted 6 tulip bulbs. Her mom planted 6 more. How many tulips did they plant in all?

_____ tulips

3. Mary picked 10 tomatoes. She gave 3 to her neighbor. How many tomatoes are left?

_____ tomatoes

4. Daniel watered 6 pumpkin plants and 6 pepper plants. How many plants did he water in all?

_____ plants

On another sheet of paper, explain how all of the problems are alike.

Cleaning Up

Directions: Read each problem. Decide if you need to add or subtract to find the answer. Solve the problem.

I. In the sink are 12 dirty cups and 13 dirty plates. How many dirty dishes are in the sink in all?

_____ dirty dishes

2. Jan vacuumed for 32 minutes. Her sister dusted for 21 minutes. How much longer did Jan work than her sister?

_____ minutes

3. Dad recycled 24 bottles and 35 cans. How many things did he recycle in all?

_____ things

4. Aunt Linda washed 24 windows at her house and 12 windows at our house. How many more windows did she wash at her house?

_____ windows

On another sheet of paper, list five ways you can help take care of your home. Explain why it is important to keep a home clean.

Number Line Helper

Directions: Use the number line to help you solve the problems.

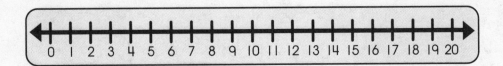

1. Lita had 8 dolls. Her friend gave her 2 more dolls. How many dolls does Lita have now?

_____ dolls

2. Pete watched 5 hours of TV last week. This week, he watched 3 fewer hours of TV. How many hours of TV did he watch this week?

_____ hours

3. Rashad read 9 books last month. He read 7 books this month. How many books did he read altogether?

_____ books

4. Beth picked 18 flowers. She gave away 9 flowers. How many does she have left?

_____ flowers

Try This!

On another sheet of paper, write two word problems that can be solved using a number line. Ask a friend to solve the problems.

World of Patterns

Directions: Read and answer the problems.

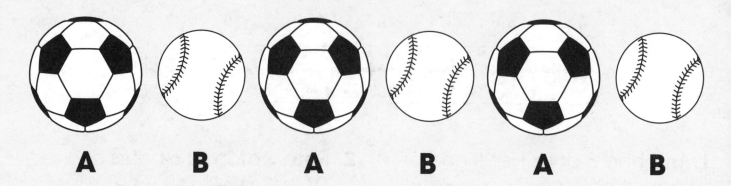

A B A B A B

1. Jared made an **AB** pattern using shapes and the colors red and blue. Draw what it might look like.

2. Pam made an **ABC** pattern using different kinds of fruit. Draw what it might look like.

3. Andy made an **ABBA** pattern using flowers and butterflies. Draw what it might look like.

Try This!

On another sheet of paper, tell where you might see patterns in the world. Explain with words or pictures.

Shopping for Father's Day

Directions: Use the items below to answer the questions.

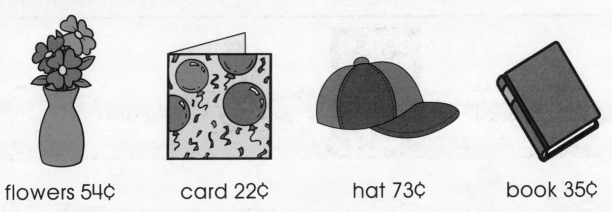

flowers 54¢   card 22¢   hat 73¢   book 35¢

1. Ava wants to buy her dad flowers and a hat for Father's Day. How much money will she need?

2. Brian has 38¢. What two things can he buy? How much money will he have left?

3. Dave had 68¢. He bought flowers for his dad. How much money does he have left?

4. Molly's dad loves to read. How many books can Molly buy if she has 74¢? How much money will she get back?

Try This!

Work with a friend to brainstorm a list of five things you can give a family member that do not cost any money. Write your list on another sheet of paper.

Healthy Ways

Directions: Use the items below to answer the questions.

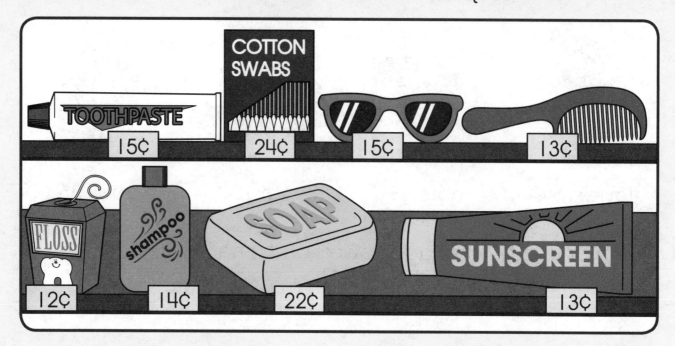

1. Kelly needs to buy more toothpaste and dental floss. She has 30¢. How much will she spend, and how much change will she get back?

2. Charlotte needs to buy cotton swabs and soap. How much will this cost?

3. Matt's hair is a mess. What 2 things should he buy to help clean and tidy his hair? How much will this cost?

4. Lily is going to the beach. What 2 things should she buy to protect her skin and eyes? How much will this cost?

Try This!

On another sheet of paper, write three ways you take care of your body.

Wonderful Weather Time

Directions: Solve the problems.

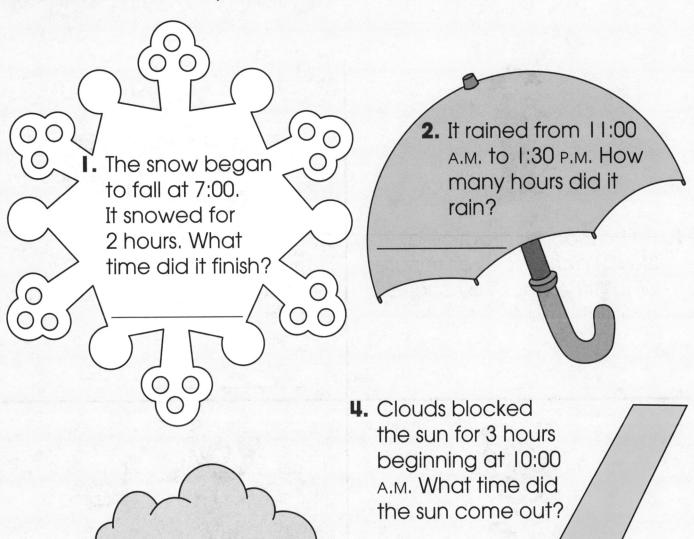

1. The snow began to fall at 7:00. It snowed for 2 hours. What time did it finish?

_____

2. It rained from 11:00 A.M. to 1:30 P.M. How many hours did it rain?

_____

4. Clouds blocked the sun for 3 hours beginning at 10:00 A.M. What time did the sun come out?

_____

3. It began to storm at 10:30. It stopped 30 minutes later. What time did the storm stop?

_____

Try This!

How does the weather change over time? On another sheet of paper, draw what the weather might be like at 1:00 P.M. on January 1, April 1, July 1, and October 1.

Time for Sports!

Directions: Solve the problems.

1. Tia has soccer practice at 3:30. Practice lasts 60 minutes. What time does Tia's soccer practice finish?

_____

2. Shay runs at 7:00 every morning. Her run lasts 30 minutes. What time does Shay finish?

_____

3. Parker finished football practice at noon on Saturday. Practice lasted 2 hours. What time did it begin?

_____

4. Miguel has a tennis match at 10:30. He plays for 1 hour. What time does he finish?

_____

What is your favorite sport? Answer the question on another sheet of paper and write three sentences to explain why the sport is your favorite.

February Activity Planner

Directions: Use the calendar to solve the problems.

February

Sunday	Monday	Tuesday	Wednesday	Thursday	Friday	Saturday
					1	2
3	4	5	6	7	8	9
10	11	12	13	14 ♥	15	16
17	18	19	20	21	22	23
24	25	26	27	28		

1. Sally went to the museum on the last Saturday of the month. What is the date Sally went to the museum?

_____

2. It will be Valentine's Day in 9 days. What day of the week is it?

_____

3. Valentine's Day was 1 week ago. What day of the week is it?

_____

4. It is the third Tuesday of the month. Carter's birthday will be in 3 days. What day of the week is Carter's birthday?

_____

Choose one holiday that happens in February to tell more about. On another sheet of paper, draw a picture and write five things that tell more about that holiday.

Math and Me

Directions: Draw a line to match each picture to the type of math being used.

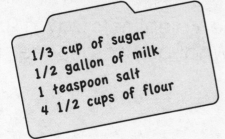

1/3 cup of sugar
1/2 gallon of milk
1 teaspoon salt
4 1/2 cups of flour

• Money •

• Fractions •

• Time •

• Graphs •

• Counting •

• Measurement •

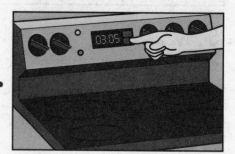

Draw a picture that shows when you use math. List the math skills you are using.

Try This!

On another sheet of paper, explain your favorite way to use math outside of school. Draw a picture to illustrate your use of math.

Answer Key

acorn

cord

store

horn

1. 2:00

2. 11:00

3. 4:00

4. 6:00

5. 7:00

6. 9:00

June

Sunday	Monday	Tuesday	Wednesday	Thursday	Friday	Saturday
			1	2	3	4
5	6	7	8	9	10	11
12	13	14	15	16	17	18
19	20	21	22	23	24	25
	27	28	29	30		

Page 10
Box 1: b, bear; d, dog; f, fox; g, goat; Box 2: q, queen; v, vest; w, web; z, zipper; answers will vary.

Page 11
Row 1: s, c, m; Row 2: f, y, b; Row 3: k, z, w.

Page 12
Row 1: bed, bird, answers will vary; Row 2: dog, duck, answers will vary; Row 3: goat, gum, answers will vary; Row 4: moon, milk, answers will vary.

Page 13
Row 1: t, s, p; Row 2: r, t, n; Row 3: n, g, x.

Page 14
Scott—bat; Nell—ball; Nick—block; Taylor—bear; Dion—train; Sam—drum.

Page 15
Row 1: box—circle, mop—circle, dog—circle; Row 2: bed—do nothing, cat—color, tub—do nothing; Row 3: gas—color, pin—do nothing, log—circle.

Page 16
Row 1: pan—color, glue, fan—color; Row 2: bat—color, wig—circle, crab—color; Row 3: pin—color, answers will vary; answers will vary.

Page 17
color: jet, net, vest, web.

Page 19
Row 1: u, e, i; Row 2: i, a, i; Row 3: e, u, i.

Page 20
Row 1: bed, mop—color, top—color; Row 2: man, rock—color, lock—color.

Page 21
Path should go through bus, dug, nut, mug, truck, gum, rug, duck, hug, brush, cup, plug, tug, up, luck.

Page 22
fan, can, crab, pin, crib, pan, fish, mitt, mat, man.

Page 23
order of train cars: cave, hay, nail, rain, snake, vase, answers will vary.

Page 25
Jean, sees, key, tree; Dean, reads, seas; she, eat, meat, beans; he, see, stream; Pete, dream, sheep.

Page 26
hive, prize, knight, stripes, kite, nine, ties.

Page 27
color: comb, cone, nose, rose, hose; answers will vary.

Page 28
Row 1: fruit; Row 2: glue, tube, ruler; Row 3: flute, tuba; circle Row 2.

Page 29
red: snake; green: bee; orange: mice, lion, firehouse, tiger; yellow: goat, crow, toad; blue: mule.

Page 30

Page 31
Apples on tree: red—nail, kite, cake, snake, tie; yellow—cat, bed, mug, sun, wig; Apples in basket: red—ruler; yellow—hat, tub; Apples on ground: red—bone, five; yellow—mop.

Page 32
flag—red; block—blue; clock—green; clover—green; blanket—blue; fly—red; answers will vary.

Page 33
pl, gl, pl, gl, pl, pl; gray: glue, glove; blue: plant, plum, plug, plate.

Page 34
1. pr, cr, yes; 2. cr, cr, no; 3. pr, pr, yes; 4. gr, br, yes; 5. fr, gr, yes; 6. cr, tr, yes.

Page 35
sp; sc; sw; st; sn; sl; answers will vary.

Page 36
color: nice/rice, sky/fly, clock/sock; went/tent, soon/moon; answers will vary but may include fish, right, trace.

Page 37
top-hop, take-lake, hole-pole, leg-egg, meet-eat, him-swim.

Page 39
three, thimble, thorn, thermometer.

Page 41
pink: shoe, shark; brown: brush, fish; yellow: tree, whistle; answers will vary.

Page 42
yellow: sandwich, couch, chair; red: trash, dish; green: teeth, moth; brown: whale, whisk.

Page 43
1. wrong, 2. bring, 3. rang, 4. strong, 5. stung, 6. wing.

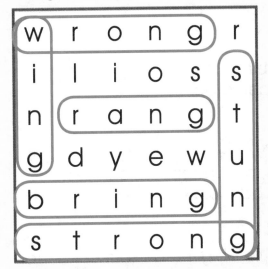

Page 44
skirt; shirt; dirt; hair; circle: bird; skirt.

Page 45

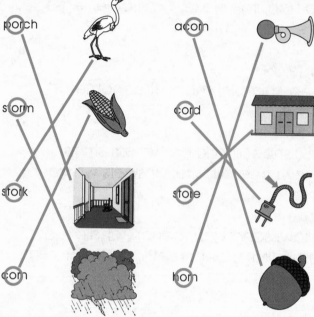

porch

acorn

storm

cord

stork

store

corn

horn

Page 46
in, on, in, up.

Page 47
One syllable: cat, bird, fish; two syllables: turtle, spider, rabbit.

Page 49
loud—noisy; neat—tidy; giggle—laugh; messy—sloppy; happy—glad; ill—sick; angry—mad; below—under.

Page 51
in—out, little—big, hard—soft, cold—hot, back—front, empty—full.

Page 53
toothbrush, goldfish, pancake, swimsuit, airplane, raindrop.

Page 55
1. We're; 2. I'll; 3. She's; 4. I'm; 5. He'll; 6. I've.

Page 56
2, 1, 3; drawings will vary but should show baby birds learning to fly or leaving the nest.

Page 57
Logan got a new bike. He rode his bike to the park. He rode back home. He put his new bike away.

Page 59
Answers will vary.

Page 60
1. r; 2. o; 3. w; row; row, row, row, row.

Page 61
4, 2, 3, 1.

Page 63
eight; web; home; insects; drawings will vary.

Page 64
Joe went to the park. Tara loves to play dress-up.

Page 65
1. true; 2. false; 3. true; 4. true.

Page 66
1. nonfiction; 2. fiction; 3. fiction; 4. nonfiction;- 5. fiction; 6. nonfiction; 7. nonfiction; 8. fiction; 9. fiction.

Page 67

1. groceries; 2. cans; 3. off; 4. clothes; 5. running.

Page 68

1. long; 2. There; 3. help; 4. can; Some dogs will play fetch.

Page 69

1. woods, farm, desert, city; 2. red, gray, white; 3. hunt for it; 4. a den.

Page 70

1. the city; 2. place them in a big box; 3. give them away.

Page 71

1. S; 2. D; 3. S; 4. D; 5. S; answers will vary.

Page 72

1. C, E; 2. C, E; 3. C, E; 4. Answers will vary.

Page 73

1. rain, wet; 2. sun; hot; 3. seed, plant; answers will vary.

Page 74

1. They got on the bus. 2. They all got off the bus. Answers will vary.

Page 75

It is time to get up. It is time to go to school. It is time to eat lunch. It is time to go home from school.

Page 77

1. cow; 2. snake; 3. ox; 4. horse; 5. tiger; 6. rat; 7. dog; 8. camel; 9. raccoon; "ILLIGATOR".

Page 78

head: hat, cap; feet: shoe, sock; hands: ring, glove.

Page 79

two legs: man, bird; four legs: dog, horse; six legs: ant, ladybug.

Page 81

person: girl, firefighter; place: school, farm; thing: key, book.

Page 83

horses, boxes, shoes, dishes, matches, pumpkins, drums, tables, bears; illustrations will vary.

Page 84

1. boxes; 2. dishes; 3. cars; 4. moon.

Page 85

1. swim; 2. sew; 3. cook; 4. drive; 5. works; 6. feeds; 7. plants.

Page 86

1. washed; 2. stirred; 3. poured; 4. helped.

Page 87

1. were; 2. was; 3. was; 4. was; 5. was; 6. was; 7. were; 8. were.

Page 88

1. big; 2. fuzzy; 3. tiny; 4. three; 5.–8. Answers will vary.

Page 89

1. She; 2. Dr. Sharma; 3. Do, Paul Brown;
4. We, Atlanta, December; 5. May,
Sunday; 6. On, Tuesday; sentences will
vary.

Page 90

1. Is, ?; 2. Did, ?; 3. How, ?; 4. Will, ?; 5.
Answers will vary.

Page 91

1. ?; 2. ?; 3. .; 4. .; 5. ?; 6. ?; 7. .; 8. ?.

Page 92

Bats are the only flying mammals. Some
bats live in caves. I love to read about
bats. Do all bats eat insects? Some bats
eat frogs or small fish.

Page 93

1. Answers may include dogs, puppies,
animals. 2. door; 3.-4. Answers will vary.

Page 94

first, last, next; answers will vary.

Page 95

Answers will vary.

Page 96

1. 8; 2. 7; 3. 3; 4. 3; 5. 15.

Page 98

5, 10, 3; drawings will vary.

Page 99

Page 100

1	2	**3**	4	5	6	7	8	9	⑩
11	12	13	14	15	16	17	18	19	⑳
21	22	23	24	**25**	26	27	28	29	**㉚**
31	32	33	**34**	35	36	37	38	39	㊵
41	**42**	43	44	45	46	47	48	49	㊿
51	52	53	54	55	56	57	58	59	60
61	62	63	**64**	65	66	67	68	69	**70**
71	72	73	74	75	**76**	77	78	79	80
81	82	83	84	**85**	86	87	88	89	90
91	**92**	93	94	95	96	97	98	99	⑩⓪

Answer Key

Page 101
1. 1; 2. 0; 3. 5; 4. 3; drawings will vary.

Page 102
9; 1; 4; 5; 3; 7.

Page 103
1. 5; 2. 1; 3. 10; 4. 4; 3 objects; 7 objects.

Page 104
1. circle 3, cross out 10; 2. circle 2, cross out 9; 3. circle 3, cross out 20; 4. circle 9, cross out 18; 5. circle 9, cross out 36; 6. circle 23, cross out 42.

Page 105
1. 1 butterfly; 2. 2 books; 3. 2 glasses; 4. 5 pencils; 5. 4 spoons; 6. 1 shoe.

Page 106
1. 3 starfish; 2. 2 scooters; 3. 3 bugs; 4. 4 cheese wedges; 5. 2 hot air balloons; 6. 5 guitars.

Page 107
1. >; 2. <; 3. <; 4. >; 5. <; 6. >; 7. >; 8. <; 9. >; 10. >; 11. <; 12. <.

Page 108

first, second, third, fourth, fifth.

Page 109

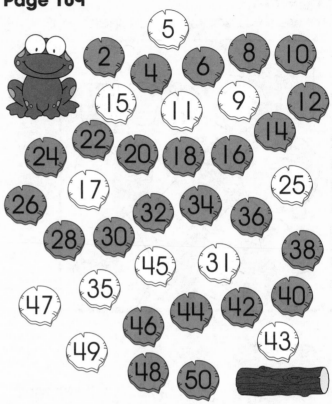

Page 110
5, 10, 15, 20, 25, 30, 35, 40, 45, 50.

Page 111

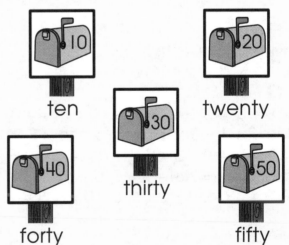

Page 113

Answers will vary but may include:

Page 114

1. $\frac{1}{2}$; 2. $\frac{1}{4}$; 3. $\frac{3}{4}$; 4. $\frac{1}{3}$; 5.-6. Check that fractions are colored correctly.

Page 115

two, three, four, four, two, two, three, two.

Page 116

Clockwise: 3, 5, 4, 3, 4, 5.

Page 117

yellow: 0 + 0 = 0, 1 + 0 = 1, 0 + 1 = 1, 1 + 0 = 1; blue: 2 + 1 = 3, 3 + 0 = 3; orange: 2 + 2 = 4, 3 + 1 = 4, 4 + 0 = 4, 1 + 3 = 4, 1 + 4 = 5; purple: 5 + 2 = 7, 4 + 3 = 7, 6 + 1 = 7, 7 + 0 = 7, 3 + 3 = 6, 4 + 2 = 6, 6 + 0 = 6, 5 + 2 = 7.

Page 118

8 + 2 = 10, 9 + 6 = 15, 2 + 2 = 4; 1 + 2 = 3, 6 + 7 = 13, 5 + 6 = 11, 3 + 2 = 5, 6 + 8 = 14, 5 + 5 = 10, 6 + 6 = 12, 6 + 3 = 9, 3 + 4 = 7, 6 + 2 = 8, 1 + 1 = 2, 1 + 5 = 6.

Page 119

13, 14, 11, 13, 11, 12, 13, 17; 11, 11, 12, 13, 13, 13, 14, 17.

Page 120

top to bottom, left to right: 58, 46, 88, 48, 75, 97, 19; red: 58, 88, 75, 97; blue: 46, 19, 48.

Page 121

top to bottom, left to right: 31, 73, 60, 46, 52, 71, 40, 58; HONEST ABE.

Page 122

top to bottom, left to right: 0, 5, 7, 1, 3, 2, 3, 4, 3, 3, 3, 7, 0, 2, 3, 3, 1, 2, 4, 1, 2, 5, 8, 2, 4, 6; yellow: 7 – 5, 7 – 4, 10 – 7, 3 – 0, 9 – 6, 4 – 1, 6 – 3, 8 – 5, 5 – 3, 2 – 0, 3 – 1, 6 – 4.

Page 123

top to bottom, left to right: 4, 2, 3, 2, 1, 2, 1, 3, 1; red: 4 – 3, 2 – 1, 3 – 2; orange: 4 – 2, 3 – 1, 5 – 3; yellow: 5 – 2, 4 – 1; brown: 5 – 1.

Page 124

top to bottom, left to right: 15, 12, 4, 3, 9, 11, 18, 7; NINA, PINTA, and SANTA MARIA.

Answer Key

Page 125
top to bottom, left to right: 32, 52, 13, 21, 41, 22, 23, 61, 10.

Page 127
top to bottom, left to right: 52, 9, 36, 35, 19, 18.

Page 129
Marcus: 3 + 2 = 5, 5 + 5 = 10, 9 + 1 = 10, 2 + 6 = 8, 5 + 4 = 9, 6 + 4 = 10, 5 + 2 = 7, 5 + 3 = 8, 2 + 7 = 9; Mona: 3 − 3 = 0, 9 − 4 = 5, 10 − 8 = 2, 10 − 3 = 7, 8 − 2 = 6, 7 − 3 = 4, 6 − 3 = 3.

Page 130
top to bottom, left to right: 10, 12, 13, 11, 4, 19, 5, 15, 6, 3, 8, 17; A NORTH POLE AND A SOUTH POLE.

Page 131
top to bottom, left to right: 25, 21, 3, 14, 59, 10, 32, 6, 27; circle: apple, bread, strawberry, milk, lettuce, yogurt; box: cookie, soft drink, ice-cream cone.

Page 132
large heart, small heart; large heart, upside-down large heart, small heart; large heart, small heart facing left, small heart facing left, large heart; small heart, large heart, upside-down small heart.

Page 133
1. 4 strawberries, 5 strawberries; 2. 8 strawberries, 10 strawberries; 3. 7 strawberries, 9 strawberries; 4. Answers will vary.

Page 134
Greens: 9 − 6 = 3, 3 + 6 = 9, 6 + 3 = 9, 9 − 3 = 6; Browns: 9 + 3 = 12, 12 − 9 = 3, 3 + 9 = 12, 12 − 3 = 9.

Page 135
milk: cheese, cottage cheese, yogurt; meats & beans: beans, chicken, fish, ham; fruits: cherries, oranges, pears; oils: butter, olive oil; vegetables: carrots, lettuce; grains: bagel, rolls, toast.

Page 136
1. 2; 2. 2; 3. 3; 4. 3; 5. 5; 6. 1.

Page 137
1. 2; 2. 3; 3. 6; 4. 1; answers will vary.

Page 138
Row 1: 6, 5, 9; Row 2: 19, 9, 8; Row 3: 14, 3, 10; Row 4: 7, 9, 9.

Page 139
odd numbers: 17, 23, 9; even numbers: 34, 16, 8.

Page 141
top to bottom, left to right: 6, 15, 12, 10, 8, 13, 10, 13; 2 tens and 9 ones; 3 tens and 4 ones; 1 ten and 8 ones; 4 tens and 8 ones.

189

Answer Key

Page 142
top to bottom: 5 tens, 1 hundred, 2 ones; 3 hundreds, 4 tens, 7 ones; 0 tens, 2 hundreds, 1 one; 6 ones, 3 tens, 1 hundred; 4 hundreds, 3 ones, 6 tens.

Page 143

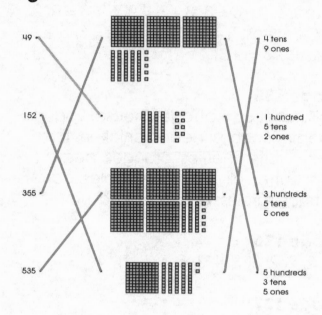

Page 144
3; 6; 9; answers will vary; 3; 4; 4; 3; 4; 4.

Page 145
red: baseball, globe, beach ball; blue: gift box, ice cube; green: ice-cream cone, party hat, cone; orange: soup can, towel roll; 1. 3; 2. 3; 3. 2; 4. 2.

Page 146
1. yes; 2. no; 3. yes; 4. yes; 5. no; 6. no; answers will vary.

Page 147
7; Saturday, Sunday; Monday, Tuesday, Wednesday, Thursday, Friday.

Page 148
twelve; January; December; yes, yes, no, yes.

Page 149
spring; autumn; summer; winter; glue pictures in the following order: spring, summer, autumn, winter.

Page 151

| | | | | June | | |
Sunday	Monday	Tuesday	Wednesday	Thursday	Friday	Saturday
			1	2	3	4
5	6	7	8	9	10	11
12	13	14	15	16	17	18
19	20	21	22	23	24	25
26	27	28	29	30		

1. Thursday; 2. 4; 3. 4.

Page 152
1. night; 2. morning; 3. noon; 4. afternoon; 4, 1, 2, 3.

Page 153

1. 2:00

2. 11:00

3. 4:00

4. 6:00

5. 7:00

6. 9:00

Page 154

1. 10:30; 2. 12:30; 3. 5:30; 4. 7:30; 5. 9:30; 6. 3:30.

Page 155

8; 5; 8; 6; 4; 7; circle: toothbrush, floss, mouthwash, toothpaste.

Page 156

Answers will vary.

Page 157

1 inch; 8 centimeters; 5 inches; 14 centimeters.

Page 158

1. scissors; 2. soccer ball; 3. crayon box; 1, 3, 2.

Page 159

1. $1.25; 2. 20¢; 3. $1.10; 4. 4¢.

Page 160

top to bottom, left to right: drum (7¢); wagon (11¢); truck (11¢); paint (16¢); shovel (12¢); apple (15¢).

Page 161

1. Sam; 2. Caitlyn; 3. 5; 4. 11; 5. 1; 6. 19.

Page 162

1. Ruby; 2. 20; 3. Ruby; 4. 5; 5. 40; 6. 90.

Page 163

1. 3; 2. car; 3. boat; 4. 2; 5. 8.

Page 164

1. 7; 2. bird; 3. 4; 4. 2; 5. 19.

Page 165

1. green; 2. red or blue; 3. yellow; 4. green.

Page 166

1. green; 2. orange; 3. yellow.

Page 167

1. 8, healthy; 2. 8; 3. 7, healthy; 4. 16, healthy.

Page 168

1. 79; 2. 99; 3. 56; 4. 48.

Page 169

1. 5, winter; 2. 3, summer; 3. 4, autumn; 4. 2, spring.

Page 170

1. 13; 2. 36; 3. 12; 4. 44.

Page 171
1. 3; 2. 12; 3. 7; 4. 12.

Page 172
1. 25; 2. 11; 3. 59; 4. 12.

Page 173
1. 10; 2. 2; 3. 16; 4. 9.

Page 174
Answers will vary.

Page 175
1. $1.27 or 127¢; 2. Book—3¢ left or card—16¢ left; 3. 14¢; 4. 2 and 4¢ back.

Page 176
1. 27¢ and get 3¢ back; 2. 46¢; 3. shampoo and comb, 27¢; 4. sunglasses and sunscreen, 28¢.

Page 177
1. 9:00; 2. $2\frac{1}{2}$ hours; 3. 11:00; 4. 1:00 P.M.

Page 178
1. 4:30; 2. 7:30; 3. 10:00 A.M.; 4. 11:30.

Page 179
1. February 23; 2. Tuesday; 3. Thursday; 4. Friday.

Page 180

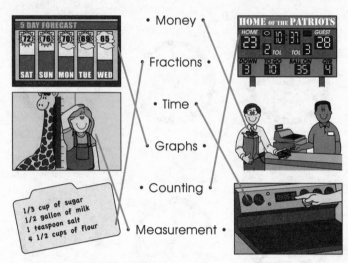

Drawings will vary.